HOW CAN YOU MASTER OR FURTHER YOUR LEADERSHIP SKILLS

THE SECRET OF PRACTICAL LEADERSHIP

The text focuses on the development of a great leader's mindset and capabilities

By

Frank E. Phillips

Copyright C by Frank E. Phillips 2024. All rights reserved.

Before this document is duplicated or reproduced in any manner, the publisher's consent must be gained. therefore, the contents within can neither be stored electronically, transferred, nor kept in a database. Neither in part nor full can the document be copied, scanned, faxed or retained without approval from the publisher or creator

HOW CAN YOU MASTER OR FURTHER YOUR LEADERSHIP SKILLS

TABLE OF CONTENTS

Copyright C by Frank E. Phillips 2024. All rights reserved.

HOW CAN YOU MASTER OR FURTHER YOUR LEADERSHIP SKILLS

Introduction:

THE REASONS FOR WRITING THIS BOOK?

SECTION ONE:

SELF-LEADERSHIP AND AN EXCELLENT MINDSET

BALANCING SELF-LEADERSHIP IN DIFFERENT LIFE DOMAINS

BUILDING HABITS FOR EXCELLENCE

UNDERSTANDING SELF-LEADERSHIP

EMOTIONAL INTELLIGENCE

CONTINUOUS LEARNING AND GROWTH

SUSTAINING SELF-LEADERSHIP FOR EXCELLENCE

SECTION TWO:

SOCIAL INTELLIGENCE OF THE LEADER

TEAM BUILDING

CULTURAL COMPETENCE

CONFLICT RESOLUTION

INFLUENCES AND PERSUASION

HOW CAN YOU MASTER OR FURTHER YOUR LEADERSHIP SKILLS

ADAPTABILITY

SECTION THREE:

THE LEADER'S PRODUCTIVITY

THE NEW PRIORITIES OF A LEADER

KEYS TO SETTING SUCCESSFUL GOALS

PARETO PRINCIPLE

GTD METHODOLOGY

PROCRASTINATION

EFFECTIVE MEETINGS, MEETINGS WITH ACTION

PRODUCTIVITY OR PRESENTEEISM?

SECTION FOUR :

TEAM LEADERSHIP

HIGH-PERFORMANCE TEAM

KEYS TO OPTIMIZE YOUR LEADERSHIP STYLE

MOTIVATING AND EFFECTIVE PERFORMANCE APPRAISAL

COMMITMENT, MOTIVATION, AND TALENT RETENTION

HOW CAN YOU MASTER   OR FURTHER YOUR LEADERSHIP SKILLS

GENERATIONAL CLASH: MILLENNIALS TELEWORK AND VIRTUAL TEAMS

CONCLUSION

HOW CAN YOU MASTER   OR FURTHER YOUR LEADERSHIP SKILLS

About The Publisher

Dear reader!

Introduction:

THE REASONS FOR WRITING THIS BOOK?

I remember the first time I had to lead a team. It was a very important change in my professional career; in fact, it was one of the most difficult challenges I have had to face in my life. At that time, I was working for a Quest International (QNET) company, where, in recognition of my performance, I was promoted until one day I was leading a team. I went from flowing with my business as an upline in Ireland to seeming stuck in my new role as mentoring downlines in the Netherlands. It was my first experience leading people. I did not know how to lead a team, as I had not been taught it at university or in any of my previous positions. Suddenly, I felt the great need to develop my leadership and other skills to cope with my new responsibilities. I not only experienced this situation firsthand, but it is very common in organizations that request my services for the development of leaders and high-performance teams.

Many organizers have been promoted as a reward and recognition for a business well done, and suddenly, although they are great professionals, they do not know how to perform their new position in front of a team. The good news is that this situation has a solution.

In this book, I present the skills that I needed to learn back in the day, when I was promoted and had to lead a team for the first time. Interestingly, these skills are the ones my clients ask me for the most, both in individual processes and in my in-company workshops for management and middle management teams. In my first book, Motivated Teams, Productive Teams, I discussed those methodologies and tools that everyone who leads people should know in order to achieve a high-performance team. In this book, however, I focus mainly on the leader himself. Here, I want to expose what skills, methodologies, and tools everyone leading a team should know in order to achieve greater productivity, motivation, and professional and personal growth. I was very fortunate, once I identified my areas for improvement, to have the training and coaching to perform my new role of leading a team. And now I have the great fortune to have clients, companies, and leaders who detect these needs and seek help to solve them.

The purpose of this book is to provide these professionals, who suddenly find themselves in a new situation (leading a team, increased responsibilities, new roles, etc.), with a guide to help them achieve better results. A guide for managers facing new challenges.

We will see four blocks:

Self-leadership and an excellent mindset. *We will review the importance of knowing oneself and adopting good habits, as well as how to manage difficult moments, failures, and stress.*

Social intelligence of the leaders. We will highlight the importance of interacting with others, communicating assertively, taking care of our personal relationships, and the impression we leave on others.

The leader's productivity. One of the scarcest resources a leader can have is time, and therefore it is essential that as we take on more responsibilities and when we lead a team, we learn to optimize every minute of our day. We will see how priorities change when we have a team and some techniques that can help us be more productive. I develop this topic in more depth in my book, Productivity for Leaders.

Team leadership. This is probably one of the most complicated tasks anyone can encounter in their professional life. The way we manage our teams can have a tremendous impact on their performance and motivation. Although I developed this topic in more depth in my book Motivated Teams, Productive Teams, here we will review the main guidelines to keep in mind when leading people and some additional concepts. Equipping ourselves with tools and methodologies that help us on a daily basis will improve our performance and that of our *teams, and we will even be able to enjoy our business.*

Unveiling "The Secret of Practical Leadership": Empowering Leaders for Real-World Impact

SECTION ONE:

SELF-LEADERSHIP AND AN EXCELLENT MINDSET

BALANCING SELF-LEADERSHIP IN DIFFERENT LIFE DOMAINS

BUILDING HABITS FOR EXCELLENCE

UNDERSTANDING SELF-LEADERSHIP

EMOTIONAL INTELLIGENCE

CONTINUOUS LEARNING AND GROWTH

SUSTAINING SELF-LEADERSHIP FOR EXCELLENCE

HOW CAN YOU MASTER OR FURTHER YOUR LEADERSHIP SKILLS

It has been demonstrated that the most successful people are those who are aware of their strengths and shortcomings and who can use this knowledge to create tactics that adapt to the demands of their surroundings.

In order to move forward, it is essential to know ourselves in depth, to know our strengths, our areas for improvement, and our motivators.

BALANCING SELF-LEADERSHIP IN DIFFERENT LIFE DOMAINS

Self-leadership is the foundation of personal growth and success. It involves taking charge of one's own thoughts, emotions, actions, and goals. However, achieving a harmonious balance of self-leadership across various life domains can be a challenging endeavor. In this essay, we will explore the importance of balancing self-leadership in different life domains and discuss strategies to achieve this equilibrium effectively.

1. **Career and Professional Domain:**

In the career and professional domains, self-leadership entails setting clear goals, managing time effectively, and making sound decisions. Balancing self-leadership in this domain requires aligning personal aspirations with professional objectives, maintaining a healthy work-life balance, and continuously developing relevant skills. It involves prioritizing tasks, managing stress, and seeking growth opportunities while nurturing positive relationships with colleagues and superiors.

2. **Personal and emotional well-being:**

Self-leadership in the personal and emotional well-being domain involves nurturing physical and mental health, managing emotions, and cultivating self-care practices. Balancing self-leadership in this domain requires dedicating time for rest, relaxation, and rejuvenation. It involves practicing mindfulness, engaging in activities that bring joy and fulfillment, and seeking support when needed. Prioritizing self-

care allows individuals to recharge and maintain overall well-being, which positively impacts other areas of life.

3. **Relationships and social interactions:**

Self-leadership in relationships involves effective communication, empathy, and maintaining healthy boundaries. Balancing self-leadership in this domain requires investing time and energy in building and nurturing relationships with family, friends, and significant others. It involves active listening, expressing needs and concerns, and fostering mutual respect. Setting boundaries and managing commitments can help individuals maintain a healthy balance between personal relationships and other life domains.

4. **Learning and Personal Development:**

Self-leadership in the learning and personal development domains involves a commitment to continuous growth and self-improvement. Balancing self-leadership in this domain requires setting learning goals, seeking new experiences, and expanding knowledge and skills. It involves allocating time for reading, attending workshops or courses, and engaging *in activities that foster personal growth. Effective self-leadership in this domain allows individuals to adapt to changing circumstances and seize opportunities for self-improvement.*

5. **Community and Social Responsibility:**

Self-leadership in the community and social responsibility domains involves actively contributing to the betterment of society. Balancing self-leadership in this domain requires identifying causes or issues that align with personal values and dedicating time and resources to make a positive impact. It involves volunteering, advocating for change, and engaging in acts of kindness. Balancing self-leadership in this domain allows individuals to contribute meaningfully to their communities while maintaining a sense of purpose and fulfillment.

Strategies for Balancing Self-Leadership:

1. **Prioritize and set clear boundaries.**

Identify your priorities in each life domain and allocate time and energy accordingly. Set clear boundaries to ensure a healthy balance between different areas of your life

2. **Practice self-care and well-being.**

Allocate time for activities that promote physical and mental well-being, such as exercise, relaxation, hobbies, and quality time with loved ones. Prioritize self-care to maintain overall balance.

3. **Cultivate effective time management.**

Develop effective time management skills to optimize productivity and ensure sufficient time for various life domains. Use tools like calendars and to-do lists to prioritize tasks and manage commitments effectively.

4. **Continuously learn and grow.**

Invest in personal development by setting learning goals and engaging in activities that foster growth. Stay curious, seek new experiences, and embrace opportunities for self-improvement.

5. **Cultivate supportive relationships.**

Nurture relationships that support your self-leadership journey. Surround yourself with individuals who inspire, motivate, and encourage personal growth.

6. *Practice reflection and self-reflection:*

Regularly reflect on your progress and assess the balance of self-leadership in different life domains. Adjust as necessary, and make conscious choices aligned with your values and goals.

Finally

Balancing self-leadership in different life domains is a lifelong pursuit that requires conscious effort and continuous self-reflection. By prioritizing and setting boundaries, practicing self-care, managing time effectively, nurturing relationships, investing in personal development, and contributing to the community, individuals can achieve a harmonious balance that leads to personal fulfillment and success. Balancing self-leadership allows individuals to thrive in multiple areas of life and create a meaningful and purposeful existence.

How to Develop Our Potential

Let's take a look at nine steps that will help us discover our best version:

Certainly! Here are nine steps that can help you discover your best version while balancing self-leadership in different life domains:

Step 1: *Identify Key Life Domains*

Identify and define the key areas of your life that are important to you. These may include career, relationships, health, personal growth, finance, family, hobbies, spirituality, and any other areas that hold significance for you.

Step 2: *Assess Your Current State*

Evaluate your current level of self-leadership and excellence in each life domain. Reflect on your strengths and areas for improvement within each domain. Consider how satisfied you are with your current balance and effectiveness in managing these areas of your life.

Step 3: *Clarify Your Values and Priorities*

Reflect on your values and what matters most to you in each life domain. Identify your priorities and align them with your values. This will help you establish a clear sense of direction and make informed decisions about how to balance your self-leadership efforts.

Step 4: *Set SMART Goals*

Set specific, measurable, achievable, relevant, and time-bound (SMART) goals for each life domain. Break down your goals into smaller, actionable steps. Ensure that these goals are aligned with your values and priorities and reflect your desire to enhance self-leadership and achieve excellence.

Step 5: *Develop action plans.*

Create action plans for each goal, outlining the specific steps you need to take to achieve them. Determine the resources, skills, and support you may need to succeed. Break down your action plans into manageable tasks and deadlines, allowing you to track your progress effectively.

Step 6: *Allocate Time and Energy*

Allocate your time and energy to different life domains based on their importance and urgency. Establish boundaries and create a schedule that allows you to dedicate sufficient time to each domain while maintaining a sense of balance. Prioritize self-care and ensure that you have time for rest and rejuvenation.

Step 7: *Build Support Systems*

Seek support from others who can help you in different life domains. This may include mentors, coaches, friends, or family members who can provide guidance, accountability, and encouragement. Surround yourself with a supportive network that understands and respects your goals and priorities.

Step 8: *Practice self-care*

Prioritize self-care to maintain your physical, mental, and emotional well-being. Engage in activities that recharge and rejuvenate you. Take breaks when needed and listen to your body's signals. Self-care is vital for sustaining self-leadership and achieving excellence in all areas of life.

Step 9: *Continuously Reflect and Adjust*

Regularly reflect on your progress and assess your self-leadership efforts in each life domain. Evaluate what is working well and what needs adjustment. Be willing to adapt and make changes as necessary to maintain balance and optimize your growth and success.

Remember, achieving balance and self-leadership in different life domains is a dynamic process. It requires regular reflection, adjustment, and a commitment to personal growth. By following these steps, you can discover your best version and create a fulfilling and harmonious life that aligns with your values and aspirations.

The five domains of life are spirituality, family, work, health, and community. Spirituality: This is the most neglected area of life. You do not need to practice faith to be spiritual. It enables your purpose in life and how you may think, feel, and behave.

Life domains represent the main areas of functioning in your life, for example, health, family, income, social relationships, leisure time, work, sex life, housing, safety, and self-worth.

Yes, balancing self-leadership in different life domains is also applicable in team settings. In a team or professional context, individuals need to manage their self-

leadership across various domains while collaborating with others and working towards common goals.

Here's how the principles of balancing self-leadership can be applied to teams:

1. ***Career and Professional Domain:***

Team members can align their personal career goals with the team's objectives. They can take charge of their professional development by setting individual goals, seeking growth opportunities, and contributing their expertise to the team's success.

2. ***Personal and emotional well-being:***

Encouraging a supportive and inclusive team environment promotes the personal and emotional well-being of team members. Leaders can foster a culture that values work-life balance, provides emotional support, and encourages self-care practices.

3. ***Relationships and social interactions:***

Effective communication, collaboration, and building positive relationships are vital in team settings. Team members can practice active listening, empathy, and respect while also setting boundaries to maintain a healthy balance between work relationships and personal lives.

4. **Learning and Personal Development:**

Teams can foster a culture of continuous learning and personal development by providing resources, training opportunities, and encouraging knowledge sharing. Individuals can take the initiative to expand their skills, share their expertise, and support the growth of their teammates.

5. **Community Engagement and Social Responsibility:**

Teams can engage in community service or social responsibility initiatives together, contributing to a sense of purpose and fulfillment. By working on projects that have a positive impact beyond the team, members can develop a shared sense of responsibility and contribute to a better society.

Applying these principles of balancing self-leadership within teams helps create a supportive and high-performing environment. It enables individuals to thrive both personally and professionally while working collaboratively towards shared goals.

BUILDING HABITS FOR EXCELLENCE

Habits play a crucial role in shaping our lives and determining our level of success. Building habits for excellence involves consciously adopting behaviors and routines that propel us towards achieving our goals and reaching our full potential. By cultivating positive habits, we create a foundation for consistent growth, productivity, and personal development. In this essay, we will explore the importance of building habits for excellence and provide examples of such habits in different areas of life.

Body:

1. ***Health and Fitness:***

2. *a) Regular Exercise: Engaging in physical activity on a consistent basis promotes physical well-being, boosts energy levels, and enhances cognitive function. Whether it's going for a morning run, attending fitness classes,*

or practicing yoga, incorporating regular exercise into our routines contributes to a healthy lifestyle

3. *b) Balanced Nutrition: Developing the habit of mindful eating, focusing on nutritious meals, and avoiding excessive consumption of unhealthy foods is essential for maintaining optimal health and supporting overall well-being.*
2. **Productivity and Time Management:**
3. *a) Prioritization: Effective time management starts with prioritizing tasks based on their importance and urgency. By identifying the most crucial tasks and allocating time for them, we ensure that our efforts are aligned with our goals and minimize procrastination.*
4. *b) Daily Planning: Building a habit of daily planning allows us to organize our tasks, set achievable goals, and create a clear roadmap for our day. This habit enhances productivity, reduces stress, and helps us stay focused on high-priority activities.*
3. **Continuous Learning and Personal Growth:**
4. *a) Reading: Cultivating a habit of reading regularly broadens our knowledge, stimulates creativity, and*

improves critical thinking skills. By dedicating time to read books, articles, or educational materials, we expand our perspectives and foster personal growth.

5. *b) Skill Development: Building habits around continuous skill development involves setting aside time for learning new skills or improving existing ones. Examples include taking online courses, attending workshops, or practicing specific techniques relevant to our areas of interest or professional development.*

4. **Positive mindset and personal well-being:**

5. *a) Gratitude Practice: Developing a habit of expressing gratitude daily helps shift our focus towards the positive aspects of life, fostering a more optimistic and appreciative mindset.*

6. *b) Mindfulness and Meditation: Regular practice of mindfulness and meditation cultivates self-awareness, reduces stress, and enhances mental clarity. By incorporating these habits, we can improve our emotional well-being and overall quality of life.*

5. **Effective communication and relationship building:**

6. *a) Active Listening: Building the habit of active listening involves giving our full*

attention to others during conversations, fostering deeper connections, and understanding different perspectives. This habit promotes effective communication and strengthens relationships.
7. b) Empathy and Kindness: Cultivating habits of empathy and kindness involves consciously considering others' feelings and needs, offering support, and performing acts of kindness. These habits contribute to creating positive and meaningful relationships.

Finally

Building habits for excellence is a transformative process that requires commitment, discipline, and consistency. By intentionally adopting positive habits in different areas of life, we empower ourselves to achieve excellence and reach our full potential. Whether it's focusing on health and fitness, productivity and time management, continuous learning, maintaining a positive mindset, or nurturing relationships, each habit contributes to our overall growth and success. By embracing these habits, we create a strong foundation for excellence and pave the way for a fulfilling and purposeful life.

Excellence Is a Habit: How to Develop It

1. *Develop excellence through practice.*
2. *Practice will make you perfect.*
3. *Achieve excellence by having a plan.*
4. *Make it a rule to stay on track.*
5. *Develop emotional intelligence.*
6. *If there's one essential habit to develop, it's getting appointments.*

Overcoming Challenges in Building and Maintaining Habits for Excellence

Embarking on the journey of changing habits requires dedication and resilience. Throughout this blog post, we will delve into the complexities inherent in habit change, discussing the obstacles that often arise and sharing valuable insights to overcome them effectively.

It's important to acknowledge that changing habits is far from a simple task, as demonstrated by the common struggles people encounter in maintaining their New Year's resolutions throughout the year. The process of establishing new routines and behaviors demands a significant investment of time, effort, and consistent practice. It is essential to remember that instant results are unrealistic, and true success hinges on maintaining unwavering consistency and patience throughout the journey of habit transformation.

It's important to recognize that setbacks and lapses are a natural part of the habit-change journey and should not be seen as failures. Embracing the discomfort and anxiety that come with adopting new habits is crucial for growth. Over time, through consistent practice, these new habits become integrated into our everyday lives.

The Stages of Changing Habits

The habit change process can be broken down into several stages:

1. **Pre-contemplation:** *This stage involves a lack of awareness or recognition of the need for change.*
2. **Contemplation:** *In this stage, individuals critically evaluate the changes they desire to make.*
3. **Preparation:** *The preparation stage involves planning and organizing the necessary steps for implementing the desired habit change.*
4. **Action:** *This stage is characterized by actively engaging in the desired behavior and putting the plan into motion.*
5. **Maintenance:** *Sustaining the new habit through repetition and practice until it becomes a regular part of daily life.*

Setbacks and relapses are common during the habit-change process. It's essential to view setbacks as learning opportunities rather than reasons to give up. Perseverance and resilience play a significant role in maintaining progress. Reflecting on setbacks can provide valuable insights and serve as motivation to keep moving forward.

Changing habits requires embracing the challenges and sacrifices that come with it. Each obstacle encountered is an opportunity to grow and develop resilience. Celebrate progress, no matter how small, and appreciate the determination to continue trying despite setbacks. The journey of habit change is a testament to your strength and commitment to personal growth.

Changing habits is a challenging yet transformative process. By understanding the difficulties involved, accepting setbacks as part of the journey, and maintaining perseverance and resilience, you can create lasting change in your life. Embrace the process, remain dedicated to your goals, and celebrate every step forward. With time and consistent effort, you can successfully transform your habits and achieve personal growth.

Building and maintaining habits for excellence can be challenging, as it requires consistent effort and discipline. However, with the right strategies and mindset, these challenges can be overcome.

Here are some effective approaches to tackle common hurdles in building and maintaining habits for excellence:

1. *Start small and be consistent.*

Challenges often arise when we set unrealistic expectations or try to change too many habits at once. To overcome this, start with small, achievable actions and gradually build upon them. For example, if your goal is to exercise regularly, begin with a short workout session a few times a week and gradually increase the duration and frequency. Consistency is key, so focus on repeating the behavior regularly until it becomes ingrained in your routine.

2. *Set clear goals and track progress.*

Clearly define your goals and establish a system for tracking your progress. This provides clarity and motivation, making it easier to stay on track. Break down your goals into smaller milestones and celebrate each accomplishment along the way. For instance, if your goal is to read more, set a target number of books or pages per week and track your reading progress in a journal or app.

3. *Create Accountability:*

Accountability can significantly boost your commitment to building and maintaining habits. Find an accountability partner, such as a friend, family member, or colleague, who shares similar goals. Regular check-ins, shared progress updates, or engaging in activities together can help keep you motivated and accountable. Alternatively, you can join a community or online group focused on habit-building, where you can share experiences, seek support, and receive encouragement.

4. *Identify and address potential obstacles:*

Anticipate potential challenges and develop strategies to overcome them. Identify the factors that may hinder your habit-building efforts and brainstorm solutions in advance. For example, if you struggle with time management, schedule dedicated time slots for habit-related activities and eliminate distractions during those periods. If motivation is a roadblock, find ways to make the habit enjoyable, such as listening to music or podcasts while exercising or exploring different learning resources for skill development.

5. ***Practice self-compassion and learn from setbacks.***

Building habits is a journey, and setbacks are a natural part of the process. Instead of being discouraged by occasional lapses, practice self-compassion and view setbacks as learning opportunities. Reflect on what caused the deviation from your habit and adjust your approach accordingly. Remember, consistency over the long term is more important than occasional slip-ups.

6. ***Seek continuous inspiration and learning.***

Stay motivated by seeking inspiration from others who have successfully built similar habits. Read books, listen to podcasts, or follow experts who offer insights and strategies related to habit-building. Engage in continuous learning to discover new techniques and approaches that can enhance your habit-building efforts. Experiment with different methods and adapt them to suit your individual preferences and lifestyle.

Finally

Building and maintaining habits for excellence require dedication, persistence, and a growth mindset. By starting small, setting clear goals, creating accountability, addressing obstacles, practicing self-compassion, and seeking continuous inspiration, you can overcome challenges and establish positive habits that lead to personal and professional excellence. Remember, the journey is ongoing, and each day is an opportunity to make progress and strive for continuous improvement.

Staying motivated while building and maintaining habits for excellence can be challenging, especially when faced with distractions, setbacks, or a lack of immediate results. However, there are several strategies you can employ to stay motivated throughout your habit-building journey:

1. ***Define your "why":***

Understand and clarify the reasons why you want to establish a particular habit. Reflect on the benefits it will bring to your life, the goals you want to achieve, and the positive impact it will have on your overall well-being. When you have a clear understanding of your "why," it becomes a powerful source of motivation during moments of doubt or difficulty.

2. **Set meaningful goals**:

Establish specific, measurable, achievable, relevant, and time-bound (SMART) goals related to your habit. Break down your larger goal into smaller milestones, and celebrate each achievement along the way. Having tangible targets and being able to track your progress provides a sense of accomplishment and fuels your motivation to continue.

3. **Visualize Success**:

Create a vivid mental image of what success looks like when you have fully integrated the habit into your life. Imagine the positive outcomes, the sense of pride and satisfaction, and the benefits that come with maintaining the habit. Visualization can enhance motivation by making the desired outcome more tangible and real.

4. **Find Inspiration**:

Seek out sources of inspiration that align with your habit-building goals. Read success stories, watch motivational videos, or listen to podcasts or interviews of individuals who have successfully established similar habits. Surrounding yourself with positive and motivating content can reignite your enthusiasm and reinforce your belief in the power of habits.

5. **Create Accountability**:

Share your habit-building journey with others and enlist their support as accountability partners. This could be a friend, family member, or colleague who can provide encouragement, hold you accountable, and celebrate your progress. Regular check-ins and sharing updates can help you stay on track and motivated.

6. **Track Your Progress**:

Keep a record of your habit-building efforts. Use a habit tracker or journal to document your daily or weekly progress. Seeing your consistency and the incremental improvements over time can be highly motivating and provide evidence of your dedication and growth.

7. **Reward Yourself**:

Set up a system of rewards for achieving specific milestones or maintaining your habit *consistently. Treat yourself to something you enjoy—a small indulgence, an activity, or a break—to celebrate your progress. Rewards can reinforce positive behavior and create anticipation, making the habit-building process more enjoyable and motivating.*

8. **Find joy and meaning.**

Focus on finding joy in the process of habit-building itself. Discover ways to make the habit enjoyable or incorporate elements that align with your passions and interests. Connect the habit to a sense of purpose and meaning in your life, reminding yourself of the deeper value it holds beyond the immediate results.

9. **Practice Self-Compassion:**

Be kind to yourself and acknowledge that setbacks and challenges are a natural part of the habit-building journey. Instead of dwelling on mistakes or slip-ups, view them as opportunities for growth and learning. Practice self-compassion by being patient with yourself and maintaining a positive mindset.

10. **Review and Adjust:**

Regularly review your progress, assess what is working well, and identify areas that may need adjustment. Adapt your approach if necessary, and be open to experimenting with different strategies or techniques. The process of continuous improvement can keep you engaged and motivated by allowing you to refine your habits and optimize your results.

Remember, motivation may fluctuate over time, but by employing these strategies consistently, you can maintain a strong sense of motivation throughout your habit-building journey and increase your chances of long-term success.

Finding sources of inspiration that align with your habit-building goals is key to

staying motivated and committed. Here are some strategies to help you discover relevant sources of inspiration:

1. **Read books and biographies:**

Explore books and biographies that focus on personal development, habit-building, and success stories. Look for authors who specialize in the area of your desired habit or have achieved remarkable results in that field. These books often provide insights, strategies, and real-life examples that can inspire and guide you on your habit-building journey.

2. **Follow influential figures and experts:**

Identify influential figures, experts, or thought leaders in the area of your habit-building goals. Follow their social media accounts, subscribe to their newsletters or blogs, and engage with their content. They often share valuable insights, tips, and motivational content that can keep you inspired and informed.

3. **Join online communities and forums:**

Find online communities, forums, or groups that focus on habit-building, personal development, or the specific habit you are trying to establish. Engage in discussions, seek advice, and share your progress. These communities provide a supportive environment where you can connect with like-minded individuals, share experiences, and find inspiration from others on a similar journey.

4. **Listen to podcasts and interviews**:

Explore podcasts and interviews featuring experts, successful individuals, or influencers discussing topics related to habit-building and personal growth. Podcasts offer a convenient way to gain insights, learn from others' experiences, and stay inspired while multitasking or commuting.

5. **Attend workshops and seminars:**

Look for workshops, seminars, or conferences related to your habit-building goals. These events often feature speakers who share their expertise and personal stories, providing valuable insights and inspiration. Participating in workshops and seminars also allows you to connect with individuals who share similar interests and goals.

6. **Use online learning platforms:**

Leverage online learning platforms that offer courses, tutorials, or webinars related to your habit-building goals. Platforms like Udemy, Coursera, or Skillshare provide a wide range of courses on personal development, habit formation, and skill-building. Engaging in structured learning can provide motivation, guidance, and a deeper understanding of your chosen habit.

7. **Seek inspiring stories:**

Look for inspiring stories of individuals who have successfully built the habit you aspire to develop. Search for articles, blog posts, or interviews that highlight their journeys, challenges, and triumphs. These stories can serve as powerful motivation and demonstrate what is possible with persistence and dedication.

8. **Create a vision board.**

Design a vision board that represents your habit-building goals and the outcomes you wish to achieve. Include images, quotes, and affirmations that resonate with your aspirations. Place the vision board in a prominent place where you can see it daily, such as your desk or bedroom wall. Visual cues can serve as constant reminders of your goals and keep you motivated.

9. **Engage in Active Observation:**

Observe and learn from people who have successfully established the habit you are working towards. It could be someone in your social circle, a mentor, or a public figure. Pay attention to their routines, mindsets, and strategies. Engaging in active observation can provide valuable insights and inspiration.

10. **Reflect on personal milestones:**

Take time to reflect on your own achievements and milestones along your habit-building journey. Celebrate your progress and acknowledge the positive changes you have experienced. Your own growth and accomplishments can serve as a powerful source of inspiration and motivation to continue pushing forward.

Remember, sources of inspiration can be found in various forms and mediums. Be open-minded, explore different avenues, and adapt your sources of inspiration to suit your preferences and learning style. Regularly seek out new sources of inspiration to keep your motivation levels high and maintain your focus

HOW CAN YOU MASTER OR FURTHER YOUR LEADERSHIP SKILLS

on building and maintaining your desired habits.

UNDERSTANDING SELF-LEADERSHIP

Unleashing Your Potential: Understanding Self-Leadership

In today's rapidly changing world, self-leadership has emerged as a critical skill for personal and professional success. The ability to effectively lead oneself, make conscious choices, and take ownership of one's actions is paramount to navigating challenges, achieving goals, and realizing one's full potential. This book aims to provide readers with a comprehensive understanding of self-leadership, along with 10 practical steps to embrace and cultivate this essential skill.

Self-leadership is the ability to influence and direct your own thoughts and actions to successfully reach goals and build a satisfying life. You may consult with others for outside perspectives and opinions, but ultimately, you make your own decisions, motivate yourself to act, and reward yourself for success.

Step 1: Self-awareness

The journey of self-leadership begins with self-awareness. This step involves understanding one's values, strengths, weaknesses, and aspirations. By gaining deep insight into themselves, individuals can align their actions with their core values and make choices that are authentic and purpose-driven.

Step 2: Setting clear goals

Clarity of goals is crucial for self-leadership. This step emphasizes the importance of setting specific, measurable, achievable, relevant, and time-bound (SMART) goals. Readers will learn techniques to define their goals, break them down into actionable steps, and create a roadmap for success.

Step 3: Developing Emotional Intelligence

Emotional intelligence is a cornerstone of effective self-leadership. This step explores strategies to enhance emotional self-awareness, self-regulation, empathy, and relationship management. By developing emotional intelligence, individuals can navigate challenges, build strong relationships, and make sound decisions.

Step 4: Cultivating Self-Discipline

Self-discipline is vital for consistent progress and achievement. This step provides practical *techniques to strengthen self-discipline, including time management, prioritization, and overcoming procrastination. Readers will learn how to build healthy habits and maintain focus on their goals.*

Step 5: Building Resilience

Resilience is the ability to bounce back from setbacks and adapt to change. This step equips readers with tools to develop resilience, including reframing challenges, practicing self-care, and fostering a growth mindset. By embracing resilience, individuals can overcome obstacles and maintain a positive outlook in the face of adversity.

Step 6: Enhancing Decision-Making Skills

Effective decision-making is a key aspect of self-leadership. This step explores strategies for making informed decisions, weighing options, managing risks, and embracing uncertainty. Readers will gain insights into critical thinking, problem-solving, and intuitive decision-making techniques.

Step 7: Building a Support Network

No leader can thrive in isolation. This step emphasizes the importance of building a strong support network. Readers will learn how to cultivate relationships, seek mentorship, and leverage the power of collaboration. Building a support network enhances self-leadership by providing guidance, accountability, and diverse perspectives.

Step 8: Practicing Self-Reflection

Self-reflection is a powerful tool for self-leadership and personal growth. This step guides readers to develop a regular practice of self-reflection, including journaling, meditation, and seeking feedback. Through self-reflection, individuals gain deeper insights into their behaviors, beliefs, and areas for improvement.

Step 9: Continuous Learning and Development

Self-leadership requires a commitment to lifelong learning. This step explores strategies to embrace continuous learning, such as reading, attending workshops, and seeking new experiences. Readers will discover the importance of staying curious, adaptable, and open to acquiring new knowledge and skills.

Step 10: Inspiring and Influencing Others

Self-leadership extends beyond oneself to positively impact others. This final step explores how readers can inspire and influence others through their actions, values, and leadership presence. By leading by example, individuals can create a ripple effect of self-leadership within their teams, communities, and organizations.

Finally:

Understanding self-leadership is a transformative journey that empowers individuals to take charge of their lives, make intentional choices, and unlock their true potential. By following the 10 steps outlined in this book—self-awareness, goal setting, emotional intelligence, self-discipline, resilience, decision-making, building a support network, self-reflection, continuous learning, and inspiring others—readers will embark on a path of self-discovery, growth, and leadership excellence. With self-leadership as their compass, they will navigate challenges, seize opportunities, and create a fulfilling and purpose-driven life.

The 5 Key Leadership Skills

- *The ability to motivate team members to do great work.*
- *The ability to build trust and influence.*
- *The ability to communicate effectively.*
- *The ability to create a positive work environment.*
- *Fostering a Satisfying Employee Experience.*
- *The ability to encourage growth and development.*

How does self-reflection contribute to personal growth and self-leadership?

Self-reflection plays a crucial role in personal growth and self-leadership. It is a process of introspection and self-examination that allows individuals to gain deeper insights into their thoughts, emotions, behaviors, and beliefs. By actively engaging in self-reflection, individuals can cultivate self-awareness, enhance their decision-making abilities, and develop a more effective leadership style. Here are some ways in which self-reflection contributes to personal growth and self-leadership:

1. **Enhancing Self-Awareness**: Self-reflection is the foundation of self-awareness. By taking the time to reflect on our experiences, actions, and reactions, we gain a clearer understanding of our strengths, weaknesses, values, and motivations. This self-awareness empowers us to make conscious choices aligned with our authentic selves and to recognize patterns that may hinder our personal growth and leadership effectiveness.
2. **Identifying Strengths and Areas for Improvement:** Through self-reflection, we can identify our strengths and leverage them to enhance our performance and leadership abilities. Additionally, self-reflection helps us recognize areas where we can improve and develop new skills. This awareness allows us to set relevant goals and seek opportunities for growth, both personally and professionally.
3. **Fostering Emotional Intelligence**: Self-reflection enables us to examine our emotional responses to various situations. By understanding our emotions, we can better regulate them and respond in a more constructive and empathetic manner. This cultivation of

emotional intelligence enhances our self-leadership by improving our ability to manage relationships, navigate conflicts, and inspire others.
4. **Deepening Learning and Integration:** Self-reflection helps us integrate new knowledge and experiences into our existing understanding of the world. By reflecting on what we have learned, we can extract meaningful insights and lessons that inform our future actions. This process of deepening learning enables personal growth and facilitates the development of effective leadership strategies.
5. **Guiding Decision-Making:** Self-reflection provides valuable guidance when making decisions. By reflecting on our values, priorities, and long-term goals, we can align our choices with our authentic selves. Self-reflection helps us consider different perspectives, evaluate potential consequences, and make decisions that are in line with our personal and leadership principles.
6. **Cultivating Mindfulness and Presence:** Self-reflection encourages us to be present in the moment and to observe our thoughts, feelings, and behaviors without judgment. This practice of

mindfulness allows us to be fully engaged in our experiences and interactions. By cultivating mindfulness and presence, we become more attuned to ourselves and others, leading to more effective leadership and meaningful connections.

7. **Promoting Personal Accountability:** *Self-reflection fosters a sense of personal accountability. By taking ownership of our actions, decisions, and their consequences, we become proactive leaders who are willing to learn from mistakes and take corrective measures. Self-reflection helps us recognize our role in our own development and take responsibility for our personal growth and leadership effectiveness.*

In summary, self-reflection is a powerful tool that contributes to personal growth and self-leadership. By cultivating self-awareness, identifying strengths and areas for improvement, fostering emotional intelligence, guiding decision-making, and promoting personal accountability, self-reflection empowers individuals to lead themselves effectively, make conscious choices, and continuously grow and develop as leaders.

Certainly! Here are some practical exercises and techniques for self-reflection that you can incorporate into your personal growth and self-leadership journey:

1. *Journaling: Set aside dedicated time to write in a journal regularly. Reflect on your experiences, thoughts, and emotions. Ask yourself questions like "What did I learn today?" or "What challenges did I face, and how did I respond?" Use your journal as a space for self-exploration and self-expression*
2. **Mindful Meditation**: *Engage in mindfulness meditation to develop present-moment awareness and a non-judgmental attitude. Set aside a few minutes each day to focus on your breath or observe your thoughts and emotions without getting caught up in them. This practice enhances self-awareness and helps you observe your inner world more objectively.*

3. ***Reflective Questions***: Ask yourself reflective questions that prompt deeper thinking and self-analysis. Examples include, "What are my core values, and am I living in alignment with them?" or "What are my strengths, and how can I leverage them more effectively?" These questions stimulate introspection and provide valuable insights.
4. ***Seeking Feedback***: Request feedback from trusted individuals in your personal or professional life. Ask them for constructive input on your strengths, areas for improvement, and blind spots. This external perspective can offer valuable insights and help you gain a more objective understanding of yourself.
5. ***Visualization***: Engage in visualization exercises to envision your ideal self and desired outcomes. Imagine yourself embodying the qualities and behaviors you aspire to. Visualize successful scenarios and reflect on the steps you can take to bridge the gap between your current self and your envisioned self.
6. ***Reflection Prompts***: Use reflection prompts or sentence starters to guide your self-reflection. For example, "One thing I accomplished today that I'm

proud of is..." or *"A challenge I faced recently and how I overcame it was..."* These prompts provide a structured framework for reflection and help you focus on specific aspects of your experience.

7. **Silent Retreats:** Consider participating in a silent retreat or creating your own mini-retreat. Disconnect from external distractions and spend dedicated time in solitude and silence. This allows for deep introspection, self-discovery, and reflection on your values, goals, and life direction.

8. **Peer or Mentor Reflection Sessions:** Engage in reflective conversations with peers or mentors who are also committed to personal growth and self-leadership. Share experiences, insights, and challenges with each other. Actively listen to their perspectives and provide reciprocal feedback. These conversations can offer valuable mutual support and different perspectives.

9. **Daily Check-Ins:** Set aside a few minutes at the end of each day to reflect on your actions, accomplishments, and areas for improvement. Consider what went well, what could have been done differently, and what you learned from

the day's experiences. This daily check-in cultivates a habit of self-reflection and helps you course-correct as needed.

10. ***Retreat or Nature Walk:*** *Retreat to a peaceful setting or take a nature walk to connect with the natural environment. Use this time to reflect on your thoughts, emotions, and experiences. The serene surroundings can facilitate relaxation, introspection, and clarity of thought.*

Remember, the key to effective self-reflection is consistency and commitment. Choose the techniques that resonate with you and integrate them into your routine. Embrace self-reflection as a lifelong practice for personal growth, self-leadership, and continuous learning

EMOTIONAL INTELLIGENCE

Managers are exposed on a daily basis to difficult, stressful situations that trigger a torrent of emotions, both for them and their teams. Good emotional intelligence can make a difference both in how that situation is perceived and how it is resolved to achieve the best results.

Emotional intelligence (EI) refers to the ability to recognize, understand, and manage our own emotions as well as the emotions of others. It involves a set of skills that enable individuals to navigate social interactions, build relationships, make sound decisions, and effectively cope with challenges. Emotional intelligence encompasses several key components.

There are even studies that affirm that a good level of emotional intelligence is more relevant to success than IQ. Findings by Daniel Goleman and the Consortium for Research on Emotional Intelligence in Organizations indicate that emotional intelligence is the most important success factor in any career, more so than IQ or technical expertise. Emotional intelligence is responsible for 85% to 90% of the success of organizational leaders. Often, my leadership development clients request sessions to work on emotional intelligence. They often present me with different situations where they are aware that, with greater emotional intelligence, they would have solved many of the difficult situations they have to face in their daily lives more effectively. Undoubtedly, good emotional intelligence has a decisive influence on the success of both our personal and professional lives. Next, I would like to expose different facets of emotional intelligence that have direct application in the day-to-day life of any manager (and, of course, of any person). What is emotional intelligence? In principle, emotional intelligence is the ability to recognize and manage emotions effectively. We have to distinguish between two facets of emotional intelligence: intrapersonal and interpersonal. *"It is becoming increasingly clear that what really matters when it comes to superior performance in management positions and as leaders in large companies is not just their resumes and IQs but also the way they relate to themselves and others."* (Goleman). Intrapersonal emotional intelligence is the ability to recognize and manage our own emotions. Within this, we would distinguish in three parts: Self-awareness: knowing how to identify our emotions, recognize our body's response, and react. Self-control is the ability to manage our emotions adequately. Motivation is the ability to generate a positive attitude that helps us face difficulties in a more effective way. Interpersonal emotional intelligence is the ability to recognize and interact with the emotions of others. It would comprise two parts: **Empathy is defined** as the ability to recognize and understand the emotions of others. Social skills, such as the ability to interact with others, The importance of emotional intelligence is on the rise within companies.

How can emotional intelligence help us in our day-to-day work with our teams?

Let's look at five ways emotional intelligence can help us as leaders:

__1. Self-awareness__: Knowing how to identify our emotions and being aware of how they affect us, our work, and our relationship with our team can be crucial. This can help us know how to detect when we are reaching our limits and act before it is too late. For example, if our weak points when we get stressed are migraines and we detect that we are starting to suffer from them, maybe it is time to start doing something (sport, meditation, etc.) to prevent it from getting worse. This self-awareness can also help us choose the right time to have a difficult conversation with a colleague. If we are able to recognize that our level of anger or stress may not be appropriate, we will be able to make wiser decisions. 2. Self-__management__: Have you ever sent an email when you were too angry and then regretted it? So, once you have identified that emotion, it is time to learn how to manage it to prevent it from having negative effects on our productivity and our team. For example, stress and anger are emotions that should be properly managed before they take their toll on us. In addition, emotions are contagious, and if we do not manage them properly, they can have a negative impact on the team (bad atmosphere, stress, conflicts, talent drain, etc.).

3. Motivation: Being able to generate a positive attitude that helps us face difficulties in a more effective way is essential, especially when we have a high level of responsibility and lead a team. There is a proven relationship between productivity and motivation, as I explain in my book Motivated Teams, Productive Teams. In addition, positive emotions are also contagious. An enthusiastic and motivated leader will most likely transmit that positivity to his team.

4. Empathy: Being able to detect the emotions of others gives us valuable information that can help us optimize our relationships with others and, of course, with our team. Being able to understand their point of view, even when we do not share it, allows us to connect better with them and have much more constructive dialogue.

5. Social skills: A leader must be able to express his opinion in an assertive way, *defending his position without offending others. Sometimes we will have to make a criticism, say 'no', or perhaps manage a conflict. It is important to do this in a way that takes care of our relationships with others. Being assertive does not mean that we cannot have a cordial relationship. Some people are born with a special ability for all these facets of emotional intelligence. For those who do not have it innately, the good news is that this is something that can be learned and trained. "Nearly three hundred studies sponsored by different companies underscore that excellence depends more on emotional competencies than on cognitive abilities." (Spencer and Spencer in their book Competence at Work).*

6. ***Self-Regulation***: *Self-regulation refers to the ability to manage and control one's emotions, impulses, and reactions. It involves staying calm in stressful situations, adapting to change, and maintaining composure. Self-regulated individuals can effectively channel their emotions and respond in a balanced and constructive manner.*
7. ***Relationship Management:*** *Relationship management involves effectively navigating and influencing social*

interactions. It encompasses skills such as communication, conflict resolution, teamwork, and collaboration. Individuals with strong relationship management skills can build and maintain healthy relationships, motivate and inspire others, and handle interpersonal challenges.

Emotional intelligence is crucial in various areas of life, including personal relationships, the workplace, and leadership roles.

Here are some key benefits of developing emotional intelligence:

1. ***Improved Self-Awareness:*** *Emotional intelligence enhances self-awareness, allowing individuals to understand their emotions, strengths, and limitations. This self-awareness enables better self-management and personal growth.*
2. ***Enhanced Communication****: Emotional intelligence fosters effective communication by enabling individuals to understand and express their emotions clearly. They can also interpret non-verbal cues and listen*

empathetically, leading to more meaningful and productive interactions.

3. ***Stronger Relationships:*** *Emotional intelligence facilitates the development of strong and positive relationships. By understanding and empathizing with others' emotions, individuals can build trust, resolve conflicts, and create a supportive and collaborative environment.*
4. ***Better Decision-Making:*** *Emotional intelligence helps individuals make more informed and rational decisions. By considering both emotions and facts, they can weigh different perspectives, manage biases, and make decisions that align with their values and goals.*
5. ***Conflict Resolution:*** *Individuals with high emotional intelligence can manage conflicts effectively. They understand the underlying emotions and perspectives involved, and they can navigate disagreements with empathy, open-mindedness, and constructive communication.*
6. ***Leadership Effectiveness:*** *Emotional intelligence is a critical trait for effective leadership. Leaders with emotional intelligence can inspire and motivate their teams, manage emotions during*

challenging situations, and build a positive organizational culture.

It is important to note that emotional intelligence is not fixed but can be developed and strengthened through self-reflection, practice, and feedback. By cultivating emotional intelligence, individuals can enhance their overall well-being, relationships, and leadership capabilities.

Absolutely! Emotional intelligence is not a fixed trait but rather a set of skills that can be developed and improved over time. Here are some strategies to enhance and develop emotional intelligence:

1. ***Self-Reflection****: Engage in regular self-reflection to increase self-awareness. Take time to identify and understand your own emotions, triggers, and patterns of behavior. Reflect on past experiences and consider how your emotions influenced your actions and decisions.*
2. ***Practice mindfulness:*** *cultivate mindfulness to become more present and aware of your emotions in the moment. Mindfulness exercises, such as meditation or deep breathing, can help*

you observe your thoughts and feelings without judgment, allowing you to respond more effectively.
3. **Seek feedback:** Request feedback from trusted individuals who can provide honest and constructive input on your emotional intelligence. Ask for specific examples of situations where you demonstrated emotional intelligence and areas where you can improve.
4. **Develop Empathy:** Practice empathy by actively listening to others and attempting to understand their emotions and perspectives. Put yourself in their shoes and try to see the situation from their point of view. This helps build stronger connections and improves your ability to respond empathetically.
5. **Enhance Communication Skills:** Effective communication is vital for emotional intelligence. Focus on developing active listening skills, using assertive communication techniques, and expressing your emotions and thoughts clearly and respectfully.
6. **Manage stress:** Learn effective stress management techniques to regulate your emotions during challenging situations. This might include deep breathing exercises, physical activity,

time management, or seeking support from others.
7. **Practice Emotional Regulation:** Work on recognizing and managing your own emotions. Develop strategies to regulate intense emotions and avoid impulsive reactions. This could involve taking a pause before responding, using positive self-talk, or engaging in activities that help you relax and recharge.
8. **Build Social Skills:** Strengthen your social skills by practicing empathy, active listening, and effective communication. Seek opportunities to collaborate with others, engage in teamwork, and develop your ability to build and maintain positive relationships.
9. **Continuous Learning:** Stay open to learning and self-improvement. Read books, attend workshops or seminars, and seek out resources that can help you deepen your understanding of emotional intelligence and develop new strategies.
10. **Apply Learning in Real-Life Situations:** Apply the knowledge and skills you acquire through self-reflection and learning to real-life situations. Practice emotional intelligence in your daily interactions, both personally and professionally.

Remember, developing emotional intelligence is an ongoing process that requires practice, patience, and self-awareness. By consistently applying these strategies, you can cultivate and strengthen your emotional intelligence over time, leading to personal growth, improved relationships, and increased effectiveness in various areas of life.

CONTINUOUS LEARNING AND GROWTH

Continuous learning is a workplace culture that encourages employees to prioritize ongoing learning and improvement. Continuous learning can happen through various formats, including formal courses, informal learning, shadowing teammates, training programs, one-on-one and group coaching, and casual interactions.

Continuous learning and growth refer to the ongoing process of acquiring new knowledge, skills, and experiences throughout one's life. It involves a mindset of curiosity, adaptability, and a proactive approach to personal and professional development. Continuous learning and growth are essential for keeping up with the rapidly changing world, expanding one's capabilities, and achieving personal and career goals.

Here are some key aspects and benefits of continuous learning and growth:

1. ***Lifelong Learning:*** *Continuous learning recognizes that learning is not confined to formal education or a specific period*

of life. It involves a commitment to learning beyond traditional schooling and embracing a mindset of curiosity and exploration throughout one's lifetime.
2. **Acquisition of Knowledge and Skills:** Continuous learning involves actively seeking out new knowledge and skills relevant to one's interests, personal goals, and professional aspirations. It can include reading books, attending workshops or seminars, taking online courses, or engaging in hands-on experiences.
3. **Adaptability and Resilience:** Learning and growth enable individuals to adapt to change and navigate new challenges effectively. By continuously acquiring new skills and knowledge, individuals can stay agile, open to new ideas, and better equipped to handle unexpected situations.
4. **Personal Development:** Continuous learning supports personal growth and self-improvement. It allows individuals to deepen their self-awareness, enhance their strengths, and work on areas for improvement. It fosters personal growth in areas such as critical thinking,

problem-solving, creativity, emotional intelligence, and communication skills.

5. ***Professional Development:*** *Continuous learning is vital for professional growth and career advancement. It helps individuals stay updated with industry trends, technological advancements, and best practices. Continuous learning empowers individuals to expand their skill sets, take on new responsibilities, and seize opportunities for growth and advancement in their careers.*

6. ***Increased Confidence and Self-Efficacy:*** *As individuals learn and acquire new knowledge and skills, their confidence and belief in their abilities tend to grow. Continuous learning builds self-efficacy, the belief in one's capacity to accomplish goals and overcome challenges, leading to increased motivation and success in various endeavors.*

7. ***Stimulates creativity and innovation:*** *continuous learning exposes individuals to diverse perspectives, ideas, and experiences. This stimulates creativity and expands their capacity for innovative thinking. By integrating new knowledge and ideas, individuals can*

generate fresh insights and approaches to problem-solving.
8. **Personal fulfillment and well-being:** Engaging in continuous learning and growth can contribute to a sense of fulfillment and well-being. It provides opportunities for personal exploration, intellectual stimulation, and pursuing passions and interests. Continuous learning can enhance overall life satisfaction and a sense of purpose.

To foster continuous learning and growth

1. **Embrace a Growth Mindset:** Cultivate the belief that abilities and intelligence can be developed through effort and learning. Embrace challenges, view failures as opportunities for learning, and persist in the face of obstacles.
2. **Set Learning Goals:** Define specific learning goals that align with your interests, values, and aspirations. Break them down into manageable steps, and regularly assess your progress.
3. **Seek Diverse Learning Opportunities:** Explore a variety of learning avenues, such as books, online courses, workshops, conferences, mentorship, or joining communities of practice. Be open

to different perspectives and experiences.
4. *Reflect and Apply Learning: Take time to reflect on what you've learned and how it can be applied in real-life situations. Actively seek opportunities to practice and integrate new knowledge and skills.*
5. **Create a learning environment:** *Surround yourself with a supportive network of individuals who value continuous learning and growth. Engage in discussions, share insights, and collaborate with others to enhance your learning journey.*

Remember, continuous learning and growth are lifelong processes. Embrace the mindset of a lifelong learner, remain curious, and actively seek opportunities to expand your knowledge, skills, and experiences. By doing so, you can cultivate personal and professional development, adapt to change, and unlock your full potential.

Continuous learning and personal growth are of great importance for several reasons:

1. ***Adaptability:*** *The world is constantly evolving, and new knowledge, skills, and technologies emerge regularly. Continuous learning ensures that individuals can adapt to these changes effectively. It allows them to stay relevant, agile, and adaptable in their personal and professional lives.*
2. ***Career Advancement:*** *Continuous learning enhances professional development and opens up opportunities for career advancement. Acquiring new skills, knowledge, and qualifications can make individuals more competitive in the job market and increase their chances of securing promotions or pursuing new career paths*
3. ***Increased Confidence:*** *As individuals learn and grow, they gain confidence in their abilities. Continuous learning builds self-esteem and self-efficacy, bolstering individuals' belief in their capability to tackle challenges and achieve their goals. Increased confidence positively impacts performance and overall well-being.*
4. ***Personal Fulfillment:*** *Engaging in continuous learning and personal growth can bring a sense of fulfillment and*

purpose. It allows individuals to pursue their interests, passions, and curiosity, leading to a more meaningful and satisfying life.
5. **Cognitive Benefits:** Continuous learning stimulates the brain and keeps it active. It enhances cognitive functioning, memory retention, and critical thinking skills. Learning new things can improve problem-solving abilities, creativity, and decision-making, leading to greater mental agility and overall cognitive well-being.
6. **Enhanced Adaptability to Change:** In a rapidly changing world, individuals who embrace continuous learning are better equipped to handle uncertainty and change. They develop a growth mindset, which enables them to approach new situations with curiosity and resilience rather than fear or resistance.
7. **Personal Growth and Self-Improvement:** Continuous learning facilitates personal growth and self-improvement in various areas of life. It supports the development of emotional intelligence, communication skills, leadership abilities, and other qualities that contribute to personal and interpersonal success.

8. **Improved Relationships:** Continuous learning strengthens interpersonal relationships. By expanding their knowledge and understanding, individuals can communicate effectively, empathize with others' perspectives, and build stronger connections. It fosters open-mindedness, respect, and appreciation for diversity.
9. **Innovation and Creativity:** Continuous learning fuels innovation and creativity. As individuals expose themselves to new ideas, perspectives, and experiences, they can combine and synthesize information in unique ways, leading to innovative solutions, products, and approaches.
10. **Lifelong Personal Development:** Continuous learning and personal growth are ongoing processes that can span a lifetime. They promote a sense of curiosity, exploration, and self-discovery. By continually seeking new knowledge and experiences, individuals can continue to evolve, develop new skills, and enrich their lives.

In summary, continuous learning and personal growth are essential for adapting to change, advancing careers, building confidence, *finding fulfillment, staying mentally sharp, nurturing relationships, fostering innovation, and experiencing lifelong personal development. Embracing a mindset of continuous learning can lead to a more fulfilling, successful, and meaningful life.*

SUSTAINING SELF-LEADERSHIP FOR EXCELLENCE

Sustaining self-leadership for excellence involves taking ownership of one's personal and professional development, consistently demonstrating proactive behaviors, and maintaining high standards of performance. It encompasses a range of practices and attitudes that enable individuals to consistently excel and achieve their goals. Here are key elements and strategies for sustaining self-leadership for excellence:

1. **1. Goal Setting**: Set clear, specific, and challenging goals that align with your values and aspirations. Break them down into actionable steps and create a plan to achieve them. Regularly review and update your goals to ensure they remain relevant and motivating.
2. **2. Self-awareness**: Develop a deep understanding of your strengths, weaknesses, values, and motivators. Reflect on your thoughts, emotions, and behaviors to gain insights into how they impact your performance. Leverage your strengths while actively working on areas for improvement.
3. **Self-Motivation**: Cultivate intrinsic motivation by connecting your goals to your values and finding personal meaning in your work. Set up systems of rewards and recognition for achieving milestones along the way. Maintain a

positive mindset and focus on the progress you make, celebrating small wins.

4. **Time Management**: *Effectively manage your time and prioritize tasks to ensure you allocate sufficient energy and attention to activities that contribute to excellence. Set boundaries, minimize distractions, and establish routines that optimize productivity.*
5. **Continuous Learning:** *Embrace a lifelong learning mindset and actively seek opportunities to acquire new knowledge, skills, and experiences. Stay up-to-date with industry trends, engage in professional development activities, and seek feedback to enhance your expertise.*
6. **Accountability**: *Hold yourself accountable for your actions, commitments, and outcomes. Be reliable and follow through on your responsibilities. Take ownership of mistakes, learn from them, and make necessary adjustments to improve.*
7. **Resilience**: *Develop resilience to navigate challenges, setbacks, and failures. Cultivate a growth mindset that views obstacles as opportunities for learning and growth. Develop coping*

strategies, seek support when needed, and maintain a positive outlook in the face of adversity

8. **Self-Reflection**: Regularly reflect on your performance, experiences, and lessons learned. Analyze both successes and failures to extract valuable insights. Identify areas for improvement and develop action plans to enhance your skills and capabilities.

9. **Integrity and Ethics:** Uphold high ethical standards and act with integrity in all aspects of your life. Demonstrate honesty, transparency, and accountability in your interactions with others. Build trust and credibility through consistent ethical behavior.

10. **Well-being and self-care:** Prioritize your well-being by taking care of your physical, mental, and emotional health. Maintain a healthy work-life balance, engage in activities that bring you joy and relaxation, and practice self-care strategies to recharge and sustain your energy levels.

11. **Networking and Collaboration:** Build a strong network of peers, mentors, and professionals who inspire and support your growth. Collaborate with others, share knowledge, and seek opportunities

> for collaboration and learning from diverse perspectives.
> 12. **Reflection on Excellence:** *Continuously define and redefine what excellence means to you. Reflect on your personal values, purpose, and the impact you want to make. Strive for excellence not only in outcomes but also in the process and the way you approach your work.*

By consistently practicing these strategies, individuals can sustain self-leadership for excellence. It involves taking responsibility for one's growth, maintaining high standards, continuously learning, adapting to challenges, and embodying personal and professional excellence in all endeavors.

Certainly! Here are further explanations of the additional strategies for sustaining self-leadership for excellence:

1. *1. **Be Clear About Your Values:** Clarify your personal values and align them with your leadership approach. Clearly defined values serve as a compass for decision-making, guide your behaviors and interactions, and help build trust and credibility with colleagues.*

2. ***Change Your Mindset***: *Adopt a growth mindset that embraces challenges, views failures as learning opportunities, and believes in the potential for continuous improvement. Embrace a positive and optimistic attitude that fosters resilience and promotes a culture of excellence.*
3. ***Establish a Common Leadership Language:*** *Develop a shared understanding and language around leadership within your team or organization. Clearly communicate your expectations, values, and goals to ensure everyone is on the same page. This promotes consistency, collaboration, and a unified approach to achieving excellence.*
4. ***Plan Your Performance:*** *Develop a performance plan that outlines your goals, strategies, and metrics for success. Break down your goals into specific, measurable, achievable, relevant, and time-bound (SMART) objectives. Regularly monitor your progress and make the necessary adjustments to stay on track*
5. ***Be Proactive***: *Take initiative and demonstrate proactive behaviors in your leadership role. Anticipate challenges, identify opportunities for improvement,*

and take action to address them. Seek out new ideas, innovative solutions, and ways to add value to your team or organization.

By incorporating these strategies into your self-leadership approach, you can enhance your effectiveness as a leader, foster strong relationships with colleagues, drive performance, and sustain a culture of excellence.

Transformational leaders lead themselves well as they practice five simple principles.

- *Learn. "Learning to lead yourself well is one of the most important things you'll ever do as a leader." - ...*
- *Know the goal.*
- *Strategize. ...*
- *Overcome Obstacles. ...*
- *Internalize Integrity.*

Self-leadership involves making difficult decisions in business rather than putting them off. It means taking the right actions, getting yourself to do what's uncomfortable for you, moving past your fears, and moving yourself through any internal resistance.

HOW CAN YOU MASTER OR FURTHER YOUR LEADERSHIP SKILLS

SECTION TWO:

SOCIAL INTELLIGENCE OF THE LEADER

TEAM BUILDING

CULTURAL COMPETENCE

CONFLICT RESOLUTION

INFLUENCES AND PERSUASION

ADAPTABILITY

TEAM BUILDING

Team building refers to the process of creating and developing a cohesive and effective team. It involves various activities, strategies, and interventions aimed at improving communication, collaboration, trust, and overall teamwork within a group of individuals working towards a common goal.

The primary objectives of team-building are:

1. ***Fostering Collaboration:*** *Team-building activities encourage team members to work together, share ideas, and collaborate effectively. It promotes a sense of interdependence, where individuals understand that their collective efforts are essential for achieving success.*
2. ***Building Trust****: Trust is a foundational element of a high-performing team. Team-building initiatives create opportunities for team members to build trust among themselves. Through shared experiences, open communication, and mutual support, trust is developed and strengthened, leading to better cooperation and productivity.*
3. ***Enhancing Communication:*** *Effective communication is crucial for successful teamwork. Team-building activities improve communication skills by encouraging active listening, clear expression of ideas, and constructive feedback. It helps team members understand each other better, leading to improved coordination and reduced misunderstandings.*

4. ***Developing Relationships:*** *Team-building activities provide a platform for team members to interact in a non-work setting, fostering personal connections and building relationships. Strong relationships improve team dynamics, boost morale, and create a supportive and positive work environment.*
5. ***Encouraging Innovation and Creativity:*** *Team-building exercises often involve problem-solving tasks, brainstorming sessions, and creative challenges. These activities stimulate innovative thinking, encourage diverse perspectives, and promote a culture of creativity within the team.*
6. ***Resolving Conflicts:*** *Conflict is an inevitable part of any team. Team-building activities can assist in resolving conflicts by providing a safe space for open dialogue, promoting understanding, and teaching conflict resolution skills. It helps team members address differences constructively and find mutually agreeable solutions.*
7. ***Clarifying Roles and Goals:*** *Team-building exercises can help clarify roles and responsibilities within the team. By aligning individual strengths with specific tasks and clearly defining goals,*

team members have a better understanding of their contributions and the collective objectives they are working towards.
8. **Boosting Morale and Motivation:** Engaging team members in enjoyable and challenging team-building activities can boost morale and motivation. It creates a sense of enthusiasm, camaraderie, and shared purpose, leading to increased job satisfaction and productivity.

Team-building activities can take various forms, such as outdoor adventure challenges, problem-solving games, team retreats, workshops, and team-building exercises facilitated by professionals. The activities should be designed to address specific team needs and goals, considering the unique dynamics and characteristics of the team.

Effective team building requires the commitment and participation of all team members, as well as support from leadership. It is an ongoing process that should be integrated into the team's regular activities to continuously strengthen collaboration, communication, and trust, fostering a high-performing and cohesive team.

Team building refers to the process of creating and developing a cohesive and effective team. It involves various activities, strategies, and interventions aimed at improving communication, collaboration, trust, and overall teamwork within a group of individuals working towards a common goal.

The primary objectives of team-building are:

1. **Fostering Collaboration:** *Team-building activities encourage team members to work together, share ideas, and collaborate effectively. It promotes a sense of interdependence, where individuals understand that their collective efforts are essential for achieving success.*
2. **Building Trust:** *Trust is a foundational element of a high-performing team. Team-building initiatives create opportunities for team members to build trust among themselves. Through shared experiences, open communication, and mutual support, trust is developed and strengthened, leading to better cooperation and productivity.*
3. **Enhancing Communication:** *Effective communication is crucial for successful*

teamwork. Team-building activities improve communication skills by encouraging active listening, clear expression of ideas, and constructive feedback. It helps team members understand each other better, leading to improved coordination and reduced misunderstandings.
4. ***Developing Relationships:*** *Team-building activities provide a platform for team members to interact in a non-work setting, fostering personal connections and building relationships. Strong relationships improve team dynamics, boost morale, and create a supportive and positive work environment.*
5. ***Encouraging Innovation and Creativity:*** *Team-building exercises often involve problem-solving tasks, brainstorming sessions, and creative challenges. These activities stimulate innovative thinking, encourage diverse perspectives, and promote a culture of creativity within the team.*
6. ***Resolving Conflicts:*** *Conflict is an inevitable part of any team. Team-building activities can assist in resolving conflicts by providing a safe space for open dialogue, promoting understanding, and teaching conflict*

resolution skills. It helps team members address differences constructively and find mutually agreeable solutions.

7. **Clarifying Roles and Goals:** *Team-building exercises can help clarify roles and responsibilities within the team. By aligning individual strengths with specific tasks and clearly defining goals, team members have a better understanding of their contributions and the collective objectives they are working towards.*
8. **Boosting Morale and Motivation:** *Engaging team members in enjoyable and challenging team-building activities can boost morale and motivation. It creates a sense of enthusiasm, camaraderie, and shared purpose, leading to increased job satisfaction and productivity.*

Team-building activities can take various forms, such as outdoor adventure challenges, problem-solving games, team retreats, workshops, and team-building exercises facilitated by professionals. The activities should be designed to address specific team needs and goals, considering the unique dynamics and characteristics of the team.

Effective team building requires the commitment and participation of all team members, as well as support from leadership. It is an ongoing process that should be integrated into the team's regular activities to continuously strengthen collaboration, communication, and trust, fostering a high-performing and cohesive team

What are the four main types of team-building activities?

- *Personality-based team-building techniques. Including MBTI, DISC, HBDI, and TMS. ...*
- *Activity-Based Team Building Techniques. ...*
- *Skills-Based Team Building Techniques and Programs. ...*
- *Problem-Solving-Based Team Building Activities and Initiatives.*

What Are the 8 Characteristics of Teamwork?

- *Clear purpose, vision, mission, and goals.*
- *Strong Communication.*
- *Trust and respect each other.*
- *Good conflict management.*
- *Have an effective leader.*

HOW CAN YOU MASTER OR FURTHER YOUR LEADERSHIP SKILLS

- *Members know their roles.*
- *Team members are committed to the team.*
- *Hold each other accountable.*

Certainly! Here's an explanation of the key elements of teamwork:

1. ***Communicate openly and transparently.*** *Effective communication is at the core of successful teamwork. Team members should openly share information, ideas, and feedback. Transparent communication helps build trust, ensures everyone is on the same page, and facilitates collaboration.*
2. ***Establish a clear organizational purpose.*** *A shared understanding of the team's purpose and goals is essential. Clearly defining the team's mission, vision, and objectives provides a sense of direction and alignment. It helps team members stay focused and motivated, working towards a common goal.*
3. ***Set concrete team goals:*** *Alongside the organizational purpose, specific and measurable team goals should be established. These goals should be challenging yet achievable, and they should be communicated to all team*

members. Clear goals provide a sense of direction, enable better planning, and allow for progress tracking.
4. **Promote ownership and accountability:** Each team member should take ownership of their role and responsibilities. Encouraging accountability means individuals are responsible for their actions, meet deadlines, and deliver quality work. It fosters a sense of commitment, reliability, and trust within the team.
5. **Delegate tasks based on strengths:** Understanding the strengths and expertise of team members allows for effective task delegation. Assigning tasks that capitalize on individuals' skills and interests promotes efficiency and quality outcomes. It also boosts motivation and engagement, as team members feel valued for their contributions.
6. **Promote efficiency and avoid micromanagement.** Trusting team members and empowering them to work independently is crucial. Micromanagement can hinder productivity and creativity. Instead, provide clear expectations, necessary resources, and support while allowing

individuals the freedom to use their skills and judgment to accomplish tasks.
7. **Support employees in building team cohesion:** encourage team members to collaborate, support one another, and build positive relationships. Foster an inclusive and respectful environment where diverse perspectives are valued. Team-building activities, regular check-ins, and opportunities for social interaction can contribute to a strong team bond.

These key elements of teamwork lay the foundation for a collaborative and high-performing team. By promoting open communication, clear goals, accountability, leveraging individual strengths, and fostering a cohesive team culture, organizations can enhance productivity, innovation, and employee satisfaction.

Why are team-building exercises important?

Team-building activities are a core component of work life. Any company invested in developing effective workers should engage in these activities. These opportunities for team bonding foster friendship and community within the workplace. In turn, this helps to *improve worker satisfaction and happiness. Around 13% of employees assert that they are more productive when happy.*

Team-building events are a continuous process. They are necessary to form stronger ties between workers and the company. When team building is a workplace staple, these are common benefits:

1. Streamline your onboarding system.

Fun team-building events are a great way to introduce new hires to colleagues and the company culture. New employees enjoy a first-hand look at how co-workers interact. In record time, they learn the ease with which superiors and their reports communicate.

These events show that a company prioritizes seamless integration into work teams. By breaking the ice in a fun way, new recruits learn the ropes in a quicker, more laid-back environment.

2. Improves communication

Proper communication skills *are a valuable tool in the workplace. The work environment thrives when employees are equipped with the right information. When communication* channels suffer, it can reduce efficiency and collaboration.

Team-building exercises can target communication between team members. When colleagues cooperate on tasks, this can teach the basics of communication.

3. **Boosts morale**

Employees feel appreciated when their affairs outside of work are taken into consideration. When a company organizes a team-building event, it sends a message. It shows that management considers workers' interests, strengths, and experiences.

Workers are likely to show enthusiasm in a workplace that champions their welfare. These exercises also increase individual confidence in executing tasks. Colleagues learn to rely on the rest of the team based on how well they handle team-building exercises. After all, if someone shows an uncanny knack for escape rooms, they're probably the first one you'll think of for in-office problem-solving.

4. *Increases trust*

Team building is often carried out with a common goal in mind. Watching how *colleagues handle wins and challenges builds trust.*

Colleagues become aware of character. They recognize colleagues who can be trusted to work without constant check-ins. They may also identify co-workers that can grow from regular check-ins and support. Team-building exercises form the building blocks for a great team anchored in trust.

5. Encourages creativity

Team-building exercises encourage workers to use different measures to fulfill tasks. Colleagues think outside the box during tasks together. Workers deviating from strict rules can encourage creativity in work projects.

30 team-building exercises employees will actually enjoy

Team-building activities

1. Two truths and a lie
2. The one-word icebreaker game
3. Office trivia
4. A penny for your thoughts
5. What do we have in common?
6. Whodunit

7. *Lost on a desert island*
8. *The marshmallow challenge*
9. *Frostbite*
10. *Human knot*
11. *Gutterball*
12. *The egg drop*
13. *Scavenger hunt*
14. *Birthday lineup*
15. *Perfect square*
16. *Play board games.*
17. *Creative activities*
18. *Classify this*
19. *Salt and pepper*
20. *Sales pitch*
21. *A compliment circle*
22. *Company Concentration*
23. *Minefield*
24. *All the news*
25. *Shrinking vessel*
26. *Memory wall*
27. *Guess who*
28. *Murder-mystery games*
29. *Bridge build*
30. *Plot me out.*

Team-building activities to break the ice

Icebreakers are ideal team-building exercises for new hires in the workplace. They help recruits adjust to the workplace and new recruits.

These events are a fun way to welcome new hires into an unfamiliar environment. They include activities such as:

1. Two truths and a lie

Group size: *5-8*

Purpose of activity: *to build familiarity between colleagues*

Time commitment: *30 minutes.*

New recruits may struggle to navigate the different personalities in the office. To ease into these interactions, companies can organize a game of two truths and a lie.

This game requires participants to share two honest events and one lie. This can take place over an arranged break or during lunchtime.

While gathered, each person presents the truth and lies. It is then up to the listeners to guess what may be true or false.

Two truths and a lie is an easy game to break the ice between workers and a new colleague.

They push colleagues to get personal, forming an easy bond.

2. The one-word icebreaker game

Group size: *4-5 people per group*

Purpose of activity: *to understand feelings towards a work affair*

Time commitment: *20 minutes.*

This game provides an informal avenue to learn employee thoughts on an aspect of work. This could be a new policy, company culture, or even the methods of a supervisor.

The one-word icebreaker game requires a group or groups made of 4-5 people. Within that group, each member is asked to give a one-word description of a work event.

For honest conversation, each group has a few minutes to discuss the reasons behind their chosen word. After discussions, each group will settle on a chosen word to be shared with other groups.

When these words are shared, they will prompt open discussion between the groups.

3. Office trivia

Group size: 5-20 people

Purpose of activity: to understand feelings towards a work affair

Time commitment: 30-45 minutes

An unfamiliar environment can feel alienating to a new recruit. A trivia session where players answer lighthearted questions can be a warm welcome.

These questions can be based on the office's preferred brand of coffee beans. Likewise, queries on colleagues that add cereal before milk, etc., are fun additions.

Office trivia is breezy, with more serious inquiries reserved for appropriate scenarios. The aim is to open up the office as a friendly environment for new recruits.

4. A penny for your thoughts

Group size: 5-7 people

Purpose of activity: to build personal relationships between workers

Time commitment: *35 minutes.*

This game provides an interesting spin on icebreakers. It requires pennies or coins with listed years and a container to place them in.

With the coins in the container, members of the group will reach in and identify the year inscribed. The colleague will then share a personal event from that time.

This activity can create a bond between teammates. Colleagues build relationships when they learn personal facts about team members.

4. What do we have in common?

Group size: *20-50 people*

Purpose of activity: *to encourage interactions between large organizations*

Time commitment: *40-60 minutes*

*Personal **employee engagement** in large organizations can be challenging. When departments and personnel rarely interact, a simple exercise can improve relations.*

The common game can be carried out in person or as **virtual team building**. Over the course of a company lunch or Zoom call, members from different groups are placed in units.

Within these units, members are to find out between 5 and 10 things they share in common.

It could be a favorite pizza flavor or a shared love for classical music. Considerable probing takes place to learn about shared experiences. This will push colleagues to learn a large amount of information in a short period of time.

5. Whodunit

Group size: 5-10 people

Purpose of activity: to improve the knowledge colleagues have of team members

Time commitment: 20-30 minutes

This game offers great insight into the extracurricular activities teammates engage in. Whodunit requires a small group of people to write on a note one interesting thing they've done. These include activities like being the *past winner of a food-eating competition, skydiving, etc.*

This note is then placed in a container that other members of the group can pick from.

Teammates are required to guess which colleague fits the bill of the note selected. They will give reasons for opening discussions as to why this may be correct or wrong.

6. Lost on a desert island

Group size: *5-20 people*

Purpose of activity: *to get teammates excited for upcoming goals*

Time commitment: *45-50 minutes*

Team members of any age can enjoy learning more about their colleagues. The premise of this game centers on players lost and stuck on a deserted island.

They share with each other one item they would bring along with them and why.

This gives co-workers an intimate look at objects and feelings held dear by group members.

Team-building activities for teamwork

Activities that encourage teamwork boost elements that ensure a team is healthy. With the right exercises, team members learn the value of communication and partnership. Colleagues can **build** trust when executing tasks.

7. The marshmallow challenge

Group size: *groups of 4 members*

Purpose of activity: *to test how creatively teams work together.*

Time commitment: *20-30 minutes*

Team members are given 20 sticks of spaghetti, one marshmallow, plus one yard of string and tape.

Using these materials, each team is to create the tallest freestanding structure possible.

Colleagues are pushed to work together on a creative, lighthearted task. But while this activity is laid back, members learn the strong effects of collaboration.

When the structures are built, players determine the winner using a measuring tape.

8. Frostbite

Group size*: groups of five or six people.*

Purpose of activity: *to encourage cooperation between team members*

Time commitment*: 20-30 minutes*

This game will require a team leader and subordinates. Also necessary are sticky notes or post-its, toothpicks, thick cardboard boxes, and a fan.

Ignoring the office or other environment, participants pretend to be in the arctic. They are being guided on an arctic expedition, which they need to survive. Team members are to build the shelter for their survival. In a democratic setting, teammates elect a leader to guide them through this activity.

The team leader will give instructions on how this structure should be erected. He is unable to take part due to frostbite suffered during the journey. While blindfolded, team members build the structure using the leader's verbal instructions.

This task will teach supervisory abilities and instruction-taking skills. Members also learn the value of **time** management during tasks.

9. Human knot

Group size: 8-16 people

Purpose of activity: to build collaboration between team members

Time commitment: 20-30 minutes

This game is ideal for large teams and can really push people outside of their comfort zones. While gathered in a circle, team members join right and left hands with a person opposite them. Teammates cannot hold hands with the person next to them.

When all members have their hands in a knot, the game requires this knot to be untangled without releasing their hands. It requires communication and careful instruction to be successful.

The first team to stand in a perfect circle with hands joined wins.

10. Gutterball

Group size: *8-20 people*

Purpose of activity: *to build collaboration between team members*

Time commitment: *30-60 minutes*

In this game, team members are tasked with moving a ball from one end of the room to another. This game can be made more challenging by including obstacles throughout.

11. The egg drop

Group size: *groups of 5-8 people*

Purpose of activity: *to promote teamwork between team members.*

Time commitment: *20-30 minutes*

The egg drop is a fun activity to determine how well team members work together. Using different materials, teammates build a structure to support a falling egg.

The team that builds a surface to withstand the fragile egg drop wins. It's, however, important for each participant to feel like a winner. Team members can discuss collaborative skills learned from the task.

12. Scavenger hunt

Group size*: 8-16 people*

Purpose of activity: *to work together to find an object.*

Time commitment*: 20-30 minutes*

A scavenger hunt is a great opportunity for seasoned and new workers to explore the company (or conference room). The physical and factual parts of the office can be understood when hunts are well executed.

For team-building, colleagues go in search of hidden facts and questions around the office.

This can be achieved with a single team of co-workers. In larger organizations, groups or departments can compete against each other.

13. Birthday lineup

Group size*: 8-15 people*

Purpose of activity: *to show how well team workers can cooperate*

Time commitment*: 20-30 minutes*

This game will begin with groups of 8-15 people standing side-by-side. Once in a file, they will re-shuffle in line with their birthdates. Team members are filed according to months and days.

However, this should be communicated without speaking. The game is played by using signs and symbols to interact. Ideally, the entire group will be standing in order of their birthdays by the end of the exercise.

This exercise reveals how well teammates can coordinate on tasks.

14. Perfect square

Group size*: groups of 6*

Purpose of activity*: to apply another form of cooperation*

Time commitment*: 20-30 minutes*

In groups of six, team members form a circle around a rope. They are blindfolded to begin the game.

The members will then form a square by communicating in different ways.

This will offer practice on effective interaction among partners.

15. Play board games or puzzles.

Group size*: 8-20 people*

Purpose of activity: *to collaborate with members*

Time commitment*: 20-30 minutes*

Office-friendly board games and jigsaw puzzles are a fun spin on collaboration. There are many work puzzles, strategy games, or icebreaker games for colleagues to attempt. Board games are usually designed for smaller teams. If you have a large group, you might have to play multiple games, split the entire team into smaller teams, or get creative with the rules.

Team-building activities to boost creativity

Creativity comes in many forms. Most any activity that encourages individuals to think outside the box will ignite their creative minds. These games call upon communication, collaboration, and problem-solving skills.

16. Classify this

Group size: 8-16 people

Purpose of activity: to build collaboration between team members

Time commitment: 20-30 minutes

This is a chance for team members to express creative thinking for tasks. Different objects are grouped together. These can be items around the office. Coffee supplies, paperweights, water bottles, etc. will do. Around 20 objects are used when playing.

In groups of twos or fours, team members will classify the objects into a group that links them all. The groups find common denominators in each item.

Each group elects a speaker to explain the reasoning behind each cluster.

17. Salt and pepper

Group size: Pairs of 2

Purpose of activity: to build collaboration between team members

Time commitment: 20-30 minutes

This game is played in pairs. Each group is labeled as a pair, e.g., macaroni and cheese, water and oil, peanut butter and jelly. Every group member will have one name taped to his back.

To find out what is written, each player will ask five yes-or-no questions. The pairs will then find each other.

18. Sales pitch

Group size: *8 people*

Purpose of activity: *to build collaboration between team members*

Time commitment: *45 minutes.*

Team members can engage in quick reasoning through a sales pitch. This exercise follows each person as they select one item from the office. For the next 15 minutes, they'll craft a sales pitch promoting it.

Each object will be given a name, logo, and motto. They'll also give a whiteboard presentation explaining why their fountain pen, sheets of paper, or office pin should be patronized.

19. A compliment circle

Group size*: 8-16 people*

Purpose of activity: *to share different ways team members appreciate each other.*

Time commitment*: 20-30 minutes*

A team can be built and strengthened through regular recognition. While gathered in a circle, team members acknowledge the effort made by colleagues. It can be anything from thanks for being a listening ear to efficiency in deliverables.

Strategic team-building activities

These exercises demonstrate how each person views the workplace. Strategic exercises target brand identity in the office. Employees swap ideas based on what they believe about the company's goals.

This opens up an environment to stay on track with company missions. New team members can review details and **key learnings from orientation** *and game show style.*

20. Company Concentration

Group size*: 3-6 people*

Purpose of activity: *to get teammates excited for upcoming goals*

Time commitment*: 20-30 minutes*

This game is a work-friendly version of Concentration. Cards containing the names and images of colleagues may be made. Cards may also have company facts like the logo, mission statement, motto, values, etc.

Each player then selects two cards to see if they match. The quickest to match the cards wins.

21. Minefield

Group size*: 8-16 people*

Purpose of activity: *to improve trust and partnership between colleagues*

Time commitment*: 45-50 minutes*

To play this game, around 20 small objects are required. This can be anything from lunchboxes to coffee mugs. In pairs of two, one blindfolded person will be led by a seeing partner. They are to navigate the obstacle course using clear communication.

22. All the news

Group size: 8-20 people

Purpose of activity: to get teammates excited for upcoming goals

Time commitment: 45-50 minutes

This game encourages team members to get excited about projected goals. In groups of 3-6, team members in a department share headlines about potential feats.

These headlines are shared as in a newspaper article. As a unit or through a spokesperson, the measures required to reach this are reviewed.

This may be played by in-office workers and members of remote teams.

23. Slideshow

Group size: 8-20 people

Purpose of activity: to apply team effort when exploring an idea

Time commitment: *45-50 minutes*

Team members select any topic of their choice. In specified groups, each idea is analyzed and presented. This highlights that team members can work together, even away from usual tasks.

Slideshow exercises also help to hone presentation skills.

24. Shrinking vessel

Group size: *8-10 people*

Purpose of activity: *to explore **adaptability within the team***

Time commitment: *30 minutes.*

The shrinking vessel is ideal for small teams. The idea is that players are on a sinking ship and are required to huddle close. Members are placed within a boundary marked by a rope. The game requires that the boundary be tightened. This requires creativity and athletic ability for members to stay within bounds.

25. Memory wall

Group size: *8-20 people*

Purpose of activity: *to recall special moments in the office and their effects on the team.*

Time commitment*: 20-30 minutes*

The memory wall is made up of key points witnessed by team members. Written on a sticky note or across a whiteboard, team members recall

26. Guess who

Group size*: groups of three to four people.*

Purpose of activity: *to build connections between team members*

Time commitment*: 45-50 minutes*

Led by a moderator, team members are split into groups. Using clues shared by the coordinator, each group will decide who may be knocking on their door.

The person knocking may be a member of the company being described. Team members may also take on celebrity personalities to be decoded.

Problem-solving team-building activities

These exercises permit team members to find unique ways to collaborate. Participants will be able to flex their communication skills and expand their problem-solving capabilities.

27. Murder-mystery games

Group size*: 8-50 people*

Purpose of activity: *to encourage imaginative ways of collaboration.*

Time commitment*: 45-50 minutes*

Here, team members cooperate to understand the clues and rules of the game. Through clear communication, the successful team members uncover the story behind the crime.

28. Bridge build

Group size*: two teams made of 8-16 people*

Purpose of activity: *to promote teamwork through challenges*

Time commitment*: 20-30 minutes*

Team members are required to practice effective communication. Either team is required to construct one-half of the bridge using the provided materials. However, each team member must participate in either half. Members are also prevented from speaking. They are to cooperate to build their design.

29. Plot me out.

Group size: *groups of 4-6 people*

Purpose of activity: *to build a rapport between colleagues*

Time commitment: *20-30 minutes*

Movie and television show buffs will enjoy this game. Here, a moderator narrates the plot of a movie. Players grouped into teams are to guess what movie or television show is described.

This provides a laid-back atmosphere for workers to relax and interact.

Grow your skills through team-building activities.

Team-building games can be a fun way to exercise new skills, build camaraderie, and get to know one another. Whether meeting virtually or in person, find a way to incorporate these team-building activities into your *workspace or next **retreat**. People will benefit from the opportunity to change up their routines.*

CULTURAL COMPETENCE

Cultural competence refers to the ability to interact effectively and respectfully with individuals from different cultures. It involves understanding, appreciating, and adapting to diverse cultural beliefs, values, practices, and norms. Cultural competence is essential in today's globalized and multicultural world, where individuals and organizations interact with people from various cultural backgrounds.

Here are some key aspects of cultural competence:

1. ***Awareness of One's Own Culture:*** *Cultural competence starts with self-awareness. It requires individuals to reflect on their own cultural background, biases, and assumptions. Understanding one's own cultural identity, values, and biases helps prevent ethnocentrism and promotes an open-minded approach to different cultures.*
2. ***Knowledge of Different Cultures:*** *Cultural competence involves acquiring knowledge about various cultures. This includes understanding cultural practices, traditions, customs, communication styles, and social norms. Learning about different cultures helps individuals appreciate diversity and*

avoid making assumptions or stereotypes.

3. **Avoiding Stereotypes and Generalizations:** *Cultural competence requires individuals to recognize that each person within a culture is unique and should not be generalized based on cultural stereotypes. It is important to approach individuals with an open mind, treating them as individuals rather than making assumptions based on their cultural background.*

4. **Effective Communication:** *Cultural competence emphasizes the importance of effective cross-cultural communication. It involves being attentive to verbal and non-verbal cues, understanding different communication styles, and adapting one's communication approach to accommodate cultural differences. Active listening, asking clarifying questions, and seeking feedback are essential in cross-cultural communication.*

5. **Respect for Cultural Differences:** *Cultural competence entails showing respect for diverse cultural perspectives. It involves valuing and embracing different beliefs, practices, and opinions.*

Respecting cultural differences promotes inclusivity, fosters collaboration, and creates an environment where individuals feel valued and understood.

6. **Flexibility and Adaptability:** *Cultural competence requires individuals to be flexible and adaptable in different cultural contexts. It involves adjusting one's behavior, communication style, and decision-making process to accommodate cultural differences. Adapting to different cultural norms demonstrates respect and facilitates effective collaboration.*

7. **Openness to Learning:** *Culturally competent individuals have a continuous learning mindset. They are curious and open to learning about different cultures, seeking opportunities to expand their cultural knowledge and understanding. This includes actively seeking feedback, reflecting on intercultural experiences, and engaging in cultural exchange.*

8. **Collaboration and Teamwork:** *Cultural competence is crucial in diverse teams and organizations. Culturally competent individuals contribute to creating an inclusive and collaborative work*

environment. They value diverse perspectives, actively seek input from team members with different cultural backgrounds, and ensure everyone feels respected and included.

9. **Conflict Resolution:** Cultural competence helps individuals navigate and resolve conflicts that may arise due to cultural differences. It involves approaching conflicts with cultural sensitivity, actively listening to different perspectives, and seeking mutually beneficial solutions. Culturally competent individuals understand that conflicts can be opportunities for learning and growth.

Cultural competence is a lifelong journey that involves ongoing self-reflection, learning, and adaptation. It enables individuals to navigate cultural differences with respect and openness, fostering meaningful connections, collaboration, and mutual understanding across cultures.

What is the most important cultural competence?

While all aspects of cultural competence are important, it is challenging to pinpoint a single *aspect as the most important, as they are interconnected and mutually reinforcing. However, if we had to highlight one aspect that forms the foundation for cultural competence, it would be the mindset of openness and willingness to learn.*

The willingness to learn and be open-minded is crucial because it sets the stage for understanding and appreciating different cultures. Without an open mindset, individuals may be resistant to new ideas, perspectives, and experiences, hindering their ability to develop cultural competence.

Being open to learning involves:

1. ***Recognizing Cultural Bias:*** *Acknowledging that everyone has their own cultural biases and assumptions is a crucial first step. It requires individuals to reflect on their own cultural background and potential biases that may influence their perception of other cultures.*
2. ***Embracing Diversity:*** *Valuing and embracing diversity is at the core of cultural competence. It involves recognizing that diverse cultures bring different strengths, knowledge, and*

perspectives to the table. By embracing diversity, individuals can foster a more inclusive and respectful environment.

3. **Actively Seeking Knowledge:** *True cultural competence involves actively seeking knowledge about different cultures. This includes reading, attending cultural events, engaging in intercultural experiences, and seeking out opportunities to learn from individuals who come from different cultural backgrounds.*

4. **Listening and Empathy:** *Active listening and empathy are essential to understanding others' experiences, viewpoints, and challenges. Culturally competent individuals listen attentively, seek to understand, and show empathy towards people from different cultures. This helps build trust and connection, facilitating effective cross-cultural interactions.*

5. **Flexibility and Adaptability:** *Cultural competence requires individuals to be flexible and adaptable in diverse cultural contexts. It involves being open to adjusting one's behavior, communication style, and perspectives to accommodate cultural differences. Flexibility allows for*

better collaboration and understanding across cultures.
6. **Reflecting on Interactions:** Regular self-reflection is important for cultural competence. Individuals should reflect on their interactions, identify any cultural misunderstandings or miscommunications, and learn from those experiences. This reflection helps individuals grow and improve their cultural competence over time.

While the mindset of openness and willingness to learn is foundational, it is important to note that cultural competence is a holistic concept. It encompasses a range of skills, knowledge, and behaviors that work together to promote effective intercultural communication, collaboration, and understanding.

What is cultural competence and how do you develop it?

Develop cultural competency skills to enhance the ability to practice effective communication in intercultural situations.

This article will help better understand cultural competence and its components. Adopting cross-cultural attitude strategies will help to *develop and enhance the ability to practice effective communication in intercultural situations.*

Working and living in a global society requires the ability to create interactions and relationships with people who are different from oneself. It is critical to know how to assess our cultural competency and evaluate our own cultural behaviors. Globalization and diversity lowered the barriers that once separated cultures both internationally and domestically (Garneau & Pepin, 2015). Cultural competency skills can help businesses run more productively and efficiently. Practicing cultural competency skills can also elevate your customer service skills. Exceptional customer service gives you the ability to set your business apart from your competitors and keeps your customers returning to your business.

What is culture?

In 1951, Kluckhohn explained culture as sharing a pattern of thinking, feeling, reacting, and problem-solving. Culture is a dynamic relational process of shared meanings that originate in the interactions between individuals (Carpenter-Song, Schwallie, &

Longhofer, 2007). In 2010, Gregory and colleagues emphasized that culture must be considered in historical, social, political, and economic contexts. Betancourt (2004) defined culture as a pattern of learned beliefs, values, and behaviors that are shared within a group; it includes language, styles of communication, practices, customs, and views on roles and relationships. Edgar Schein (2010) described a culture as "the shared beliefs, values, and assumptions of a group of people who learn from one another and teach others that their behaviors, attitudes, and perspectives are the correct ways to think, act, and feel." Psychologists argue that unfamiliar cultures negatively affect an individual's sense-making mechanisms and determine their behavioral responses. As a result, individuals cannot accurately perceive, interpret, explain, and predict the behavior of people with different cultural backgrounds (Muzychenko, 2008).

What is cultural intelligence?

Cultural intelligence is the ability to interpret a stranger's behavior the way a stranger's compatriots would (Muzychenko 2008). For example, if employees don't feel as if their manager understands or respects their culture, *they may find it hard to trust the leader or work as a team.*

What is cultural competence?

Current research on cultural competence focuses on sensitivity to cross-cultural differences and the ability to adapt to other cultural environments (e.g., Hansen, Pepitone-Arreola-Rockwell, & Greene, 2000), or reflective awareness of cultural influences on one's thoughts and behaviors (Chao, Okazaki, & Hong, 2011). Muzychenko (2008) defined cultural competence as the appropriateness and effectiveness of one's behavior in an alien cultural environment. Wilson, Ward, and Fischer (2013) defined cultural competence as "the acquisition and maintenance of culture-specific skills" for very practical reasons:

- *function effectively within a new cultural context.*
- *interact effectively with people from different cultural backgrounds.*

Williams (2001) defined cultural competence as "the ability of individuals and systems to work or respond effectively across cultures in a way that acknowledges and respects the culture of the person or organization being served."

Why do we need to develop cultural competence?

Developing cultural competence helps us understand, communicate with, and effectively interact with people across cultures. It gives us the ability to compare different cultures with our own and better understand the differences. Unconsciously, we bring our own cultural frame of interpretation to any situation. This is not to say that culture alone determines how one interprets a situation. One's own unique history and personality also play an important role (Hofstede, 2002).

How do we develop an attitude and components of cultural competence?

Developing cross-cultural attitudes allows one to develop skills for better engaging with people from all kinds of cultures. Cross-cultural skills are demonstrated through the ability to communicate with respect, recognize others' values, accept knowledge, skills, and talents, and tolerate, engage, and celebrate the success of others. Deardorff defined competence as "the ability to communicate effectively and appropriately in intercultural situations based on one's intercultural knowledge, skills, and attitudes" (Deardorff,

2006, pp. 247-248). We adopted Deardorff's (2006) cross-cultural attitude strategies that help you develop and enhance one's ability to practice effective communication in intercultural situations:

- **Practice openness** by demonstrating acceptance of differences.
- **Be flexible** by demonstrating acceptance of ambiguity.
- **Demonstrate humility** through suspension of judgment and the ability to learn.
- **Be sensitive to others** by appreciating cultural differences.
- **Show a spirit of adventure** by showing curiosity and seeing opportunities in different situations.
- **Use a sense of humor** through the ability to laugh at ourselves.
- **Practice positive change or action** by demonstrating a successful interaction with the identified culture.

Borchum (2002) described cultural competence as "a non-linear dynamic process that is never-ending and ever-expanding. It is built on increases in knowledge and skill development related to its attributes," p. 5. We synthesized and adopted Williams's (2001) and Martin and

Vaughn's (2007) studies that can assist in a better understanding of components of cultural competency. These attributes will guide you in developing cultural competence:

- *Self-knowledge and awareness about one's own culture.*
- *Awareness of one's own cultural worldview.*
- *Experience and knowledge of different cultural practices.*
- *Attitude toward cultural differences.*

In conclusion, our global society necessitates interactions and relationships with people who are different from ourselves. By developing one's own cultural competence, productivity and efficiency may increase, which in turn may improve one's customer service skills. Customers who feel valued and understood will return for repeat business.

CONFLICT RESOLUTION

Conflict resolution refers to the process of addressing and resolving disputes, disagreements, or conflicts that arise between individuals or groups. It involves finding a mutually acceptable solution that satisfies the interests and needs of all parties involved while promoting understanding, collaboration, and maintaining positive relationships.

Here are the key elements and steps involved in conflict resolution:

1. ***Identify the Conflict:*** *The first step is to recognize and acknowledge that a conflict exists. Clearly define the issue or problem that is causing the conflict, ensuring that all parties involved have a shared understanding of the situation.*
2. ***Understand Perspectives:*** *Encourage open and honest communication to gain a deeper understanding of each party's perspective, interests, and concerns. Actively listen to all parties involved, allowing them to express their viewpoints without interruption or judgment. This step helps in building empathy and promoting a sense of being heard and understood.*
3. ***Seek common ground:*** *Look for areas of agreement or shared interests among the parties involved. Identifying common ground helps to establish a foundation for finding a mutually beneficial solution. It is important to focus on shared goals and values to foster collaboration rather than getting stuck on differences.*
4. ***Generate Options:*** *Brainstorm and explore potential solutions to the conflict. Encourage all parties to contribute ideas without evaluation or criticism. Aim for a wide range of*

options that address the underlying needs and interests of all parties involved. This step promotes creativity and widens the possibilities for resolution.
5. **Evaluate and Select Solutions:** Evaluate each option based on its feasibility, effectiveness, and ability to meet the interests of all parties. Consider the potential consequences and impact of each solution. Collaboratively select the solution that is mutually agreeable and satisfies the needs and concerns of all parties involved.
6. **Implement the solution:** Develop a plan of action to implement the chosen solution. Clearly define the roles, responsibilities, and timelines for each party. Ensure that everyone involved understands their part in the resolution process.
7. **Review and Reflect:** After the solution has been implemented, it is important to assess its effectiveness and monitor its progress. Regularly review and reflect on the outcome, making adjustments as necessary. This step helps to ensure the long-term sustainability of the resolution and offers an opportunity for continuous improvement.

8. ***Maintain Positive Relationships:*** *Conflict resolution should aim to preserve or strengthen the relationships between the parties involved. Encourage open and respectful communication moving forward, fostering a culture of understanding, collaboration, and trust. Recognize that conflicts may arise again in the future, and maintaining positive relationships helps in addressing them constructively.*

Effective conflict resolution requires active listening, empathy, effective communication, and a willingness to find common ground. It is important to approach conflicts as opportunities for growth, learning, and strengthening relationships, rather than as destructive or negative experiences. By promoting open dialogue, understanding perspectives, and seeking mutually beneficial solutions, conflicts can be resolved in a constructive manner.

The article outlines five different approaches to conflict management and describes the situations in which they are most appropriate:

1. ***Accommodation**: The accommodation approach to conflict management involves prioritizing the needs and interests of the other party over one's own. It is a lose-lose situation where one party willingly concedes or gives in to the demands or preferences of the other. This approach is appropriate when the issue at hand is not of high importance to the accommodating party or when maintaining harmony and preserving relationships are considered more important than personal gains.*
2. ***Compromise**: Compromise is a conflict management approach where both parties involved make concessions and reach a middle ground. In this approach, each party gives up something in order to reach a mutually acceptable solution. Compromise is appropriate when there are time constraints, when the issue is of moderate importance to both parties, or when maintaining a fair and balanced outcome is desired.*
3. ***Avoidance**: The avoidance approach involves sidestepping or ignoring the conflict altogether. This may involve withdrawing from the situation, postponing discussions, or simply avoiding any confrontation. Avoidance*

can be appropriate in situations where the conflict is minor, when emotions are high and need time to cool down, or when addressing the conflict would be unproductive or detrimental to relationships. However, prolonged avoidance may lead to unresolved issues and potential escalation.

4. **Competition**: *The competition approach to conflict management is characterized by a win-lose mentality, where one party seeks to assert their own interests and achieve their desired outcome at the expense of the other party. This approach is appropriate when prompt and decisive action is required or when there are issues of high importance where one party's goals must take precedence over the other's. However, excessive competition can damage relationships and hinder long-term cooperation.*

5. **Collaboration**: *Collaboration is an approach that focuses on finding a win-win solution by actively involving all parties in problem-solving. It emphasizes open communication, active listening, and joint decision-making. Collaboration is appropriate in complex or significant conflicts where multiple*

perspectives and expertise are needed and where maintaining relationships and fostering long-term cooperation are important goals.

It's important to note that the appropriateness of each approach may vary depending on the specific context and the nature of the conflict. The choice of approach should be based on a careful assessment of the situation, the desired outcomes, and the impact on relationships and long-term cooperation.

INFLUENCES AND PERSUASION

Influences and persuasion are concepts that pertain to the ability to affect and change the attitudes, beliefs, behaviors, or decisions of others. They involve employing various strategies and techniques to convince or sway individuals or groups towards a particular point of view or course of action.

Influences refer to the factors or sources that shape or mold someone's thoughts, opinions, or actions. These influences can come from various external and internal sources, such as:

1. ***Social Influences:*** *Social influences encompass the impact of other people, groups, or society as a whole on an individual's attitudes or behaviors. This includes factors like peer pressure, conformity to societal norms, cultural values, and social expectations.*
2. ***Authority and Power:*** *Authority figures, leaders, or individuals in positions of power can exert influence through their status, expertise, or ability to reward or punish. Their guidance, directives, or credibility may sway others to adopt their perspectives or comply with their requests.*
3. ***Personal Values and Beliefs:*** *An individual's own values, beliefs, and*

personal experiences can significantly influence their attitudes and decisions. These internal influences shape their perception of the world and can impact their susceptibility to external persuasive attempts.

4. **Media and Advertising**: Mass media, including television, radio, print, and digital platforms, have a powerful influence on shaping public opinion and consumer behaviors. Advertising, propaganda, and persuasive messaging can sway individuals by appealing to their emotions, desires, or aspirations.

Persuasion, on the other hand, refers to the deliberate efforts and strategies employed to convince others to adopt a certain viewpoint, belief, or behavior. It involves utilizing various techniques to influence the attitudes or decisions of others. Some common persuasive techniques include the following:

1. **Appeals to Emotion**: Persuaders often use emotional appeals to evoke specific feelings in their audience, such as fear, happiness, guilt, or empathy. Emotional appeals can be powerful in influencing decision-making processes.

2. ***Credibility and Authority:*** *Establishing credibility and expertise in a particular domain can enhance persuasiveness. People are more likely to be persuaded by individuals or sources they perceive as knowledgeable, trustworthy, or credible.*
3. ***Logical Reasoning:*** *Presenting logical arguments, evidence, or data to support a particular viewpoint can be persuasive. This includes using facts, statistics, analogies, or cause-and-effect reasoning to make a compelling case.*
4. ***Social proof:*** *Demonstrating that others, especially those who are similar or admired, hold a particular belief or engage in a specific behavior, can be persuasive. People often look to others for cues on how to think, feel, or act, so highlighting social consensus can influence decision-making.*
5. ***Reciprocity and Incentives:*** *Offering incentives, rewards, or reciprocal favors can influence individuals to comply with a request or adopt a desired behavior. The principle of reciprocity suggests that people feel obligated to repay acts of kindness or favors.*

It's important to note that influence and persuasion can be used ethically or unethically. Ethical persuasion respects the autonomy and well-being of others, fosters informed decision-making, and allows for open dialogue and debate. Unethical persuasion involves manipulation, deception, or coercion and disregards the rights and well-being of others.

Understanding influences and persuasion can help individuals critically evaluate and respond to persuasive attempts, as well as use persuasive techniques ethically and effectively in their own communication and advocacy efforts.

What is the difference between influence and convincing?

The terms "influence" and "convince" both involve the act of affecting or persuading others, but they differ in their approaches and outcomes.

1. *Influence: Influence refers to the ability to have an impact on someone's attitudes, beliefs, behaviors, or decisions. It involves shaping or guiding their thinking or actions by appealing to their emotions, values, or interests.*

Influence can be achieved through various means, such as providing information, offering guidance, setting an example, or leveraging social dynamics. The goal of influence is to shape or steer someone's perspective or behavior without necessarily aiming for complete agreement or persuasion. Influence focuses on creating a favorable environment or context that encourages individuals to adopt a particular viewpoint or take a specific action.

2. *Convince: Convincing, on the other hand, involves presenting arguments, evidence, or reasoning to persuade someone to adopt a specific belief, opinion, or course of action. It focuses on providing compelling and logical reasons that lead someone to agree with a particular viewpoint. Convincing often involves active persuasion, where the persuader aims to overcome objections or counterarguments by presenting a strong case. The goal of convincing is to change someone's mind or position by offering convincing evidence or arguments that lead to agreement or acceptance.*

In summary, influence is broader in scope and aims to shape or guide someone's thinking or behavior, while convincing specifically focuses on persuading someone to adopt a particular viewpoint or course of action through logical reasoning and evidence. Influence may not necessarily result in complete agreement or persuasion, while convincing seeks to achieve agreement or acceptance of a specific position or belief.

Examples of influence and persuasion in everyday life. Advertisements: We see many ads on TV, radio, and even on our phones and laptops. These ads influence our decision to buy their products. Political Campaigns: Very important decisions, like giving our vote, are influenced by the campaigns of political leaders.

ADAPTABILITY

Adaptability refers to the ability to adjust, change, or modify one's thoughts, behaviors, or strategies in response to changing circumstances, new information, or unexpected situations. It involves being flexible, open-minded, and willing to embrace and navigate through change.

Here are some key aspects and characteristics of adaptability:

1. **Flexibility**: Adaptability requires being open to different perspectives, ideas, and approaches. It involves being willing to modify plans or strategies and being receptive to alternative solutions or ways of doing things. Flexibility allows individuals to adapt their thinking and behaviors to fit new or challenging situations.
2. **Resilience**: Adaptability is closely tied to resilience, which is the ability to bounce back and recover from setbacks or adversity. Resilient individuals are better equipped to handle change and uncertainty, as they can quickly adjust their mindset and approach to overcome challenges.
3. **Learning Agility:** Adaptability involves a mindset of continuous learning and growth. It requires being receptive to new information, seeking opportunities

for self-improvement, and being willing to acquire new skills or knowledge. Learning agility enables individuals to adapt and thrive in rapidly changing environments.
4. **Problem-Solving:** Adaptable individuals are skilled problem solvers. They can assess situations, identify obstacles or barriers, and generate creative solutions. They are not easily deterred by setbacks and can navigate through challenges by adjusting their strategies and approaches as needed.
5. **Open-mindedness**: Adaptability requires being open-minded and receptive to new ideas, perspectives, and feedback. It involves being willing to challenge one's own assumptions and beliefs, as well as being open to alternative viewpoints. Open-mindedness allows for greater flexibility in adapting to changing circumstances.
6. **Emotional Intelligence:** Emotional intelligence plays a role in adaptability. It involves being self-aware, understanding one's own emotions, and being able to manage them effectively. Additionally, emotional intelligence includes empathy and understanding the emotions of others, which can facilitate

collaboration and adaptability in interpersonal relationships.

7. ***Proactivity****: Adaptable individuals tend to be proactive rather than reactive. They anticipate change, seek opportunities for growth, and take initiative to prepare for and navigate through transitions. Proactivity enables individuals to stay ahead of the curve and be better prepared for unexpected situations.*

Adaptability is a valuable skill in various areas of life, including personal relationships, work environments, and problem-solving scenarios. It allows individuals to navigate uncertainty, embrace change, and thrive in dynamic and evolving situations. By cultivating adaptability, individuals can broaden their perspectives, grow personally and professionally, and effectively respond to the challenges and opportunities that come their way.

Examples of adaptability include flexibility, learning new skills, problem-solving, effective communication, embracing change, and multitasking. Adaptable employees are more productive, efficient, and effective in their roles. Take on new roles and responsibilities. Suggest and implement improvements.

What are some examples of adaptability in the workplace?

In the workplace, adaptability manifests in various ways.

Here are some examples of how adaptability can be demonstrated in work settings:

1. ***Handling Change:*** *Adaptability involves being able to navigate and embrace organizational changes such as restructuring, new processes, or technological advancements. Adaptable employees are open to change, quickly adjust their workflow or priorities, and actively seek out ways to incorporate new practices or tools.*
2. ***Shifting Priorities:*** *In dynamic work environments, priorities can shift unexpectedly. Adaptable individuals are able to reprioritize their tasks and projects efficiently, focusing on what is most important in the given circumstances. They are flexible in reallocating their time and resources to meet changing needs.*
3. ***Learning New Skills:*** *Adaptability includes a willingness to learn and*

acquire new skills or knowledge. In response to evolving job requirements or industry trends, adaptable employees proactively seek training opportunities, attend workshops, or engage in self-study to develop the necessary competencies for their roles.

4. **Collaborating with Diverse Teams:** *Adaptable individuals excel at collaborating with colleagues from diverse backgrounds, perspectives, and working styles. They are open to different viewpoints, can adjust their communication style to interact effectively with others, and are willing to compromise and find common ground to achieve shared goals.*

5. **Problem-Solving:** *Adaptable employees are resourceful problem solvers. When faced with unexpected challenges or obstacles, they remain calm, analyze the situation, and generate creative solutions. They are willing to explore alternative approaches and adapt their strategies to address emerging problems.*

6. **Embracing New Roles:** *In dynamic work environments, employees may be required to take on new responsibilities or switch roles. Adaptable individuals*

readily embrace such changes, demonstrating a willingness to step outside their comfort zones and quickly acquire the necessary skills and knowledge for their new roles.
7. **Adapting Communication Styles:** Effective communication is essential in the workplace. Adaptable individuals are skilled at adjusting their communication style to suit different audiences and situations. They can articulate ideas clearly, actively listen to others, and adapt their approach to ensure effective collaboration and understanding.
8. **Managing Ambiguity:** Adaptable employees are comfortable dealing with ambiguity and uncertainty. They can work with incomplete information, make informed decisions, and adjust their plans as more clarity emerges. They remain focused and proactive in ambiguous situations, seeking solutions despite limited guidance.

These examples illustrate how adaptability in the workplace enables employees to navigate change, foster collaboration, problem-solve effectively, and continuously learn and grow. By demonstrating adaptability, individuals contribute to a resilient and agile work *environment that can thrive in the face of challenges and embrace opportunities for innovation and growth.*

SECTION THREE:

THE LEADER'S PRODUCTIVITY

THE NEW PRIORITIES OF A LEADER

KEYS TO SETTING SUCCESSFUL GOALS

PARETO PRINCIPLE

GTD METHODOLOGY

PROCRASTINATION

EFFECTIVE MEETINGS, MEETINGS WITH ACTION

PRODUCTIVITY OR PRESENTEEISM?

THE NEW PRIORITIES OF A LEADER

The new priorities of a leader in today's evolving landscape often reflect the changing needs and expectations of organizations, employees, and stakeholders. Here are some key priorities that leaders are increasingly focusing on:

1. **Emphasizing Purpose and Values:** Leaders are recognizing the importance of establishing a clear sense of purpose and values for their organizations. They prioritize defining and communicating a

compelling vision that inspires and aligns employees. By fostering a strong sense of purpose, leaders can drive employee engagement, attract top talent, and create a positive impact on society.

2. **Nurturing a Culture of Inclusivity and Diversity:** *Inclusive leadership has become a critical priority. Leaders are committed to creating diverse and inclusive work environments where individuals from different backgrounds, cultures, and perspectives feel valued and can contribute their unique insights. They actively promote diversity and equality, ensuring equal opportunities for all employees.*

3. **Fostering Employee Well-Being:** *Leaders are increasingly attuned to the well-being and work-life balance of their employees. They prioritize creating a supportive and healthy work environment that promotes physical, mental, and emotional well-being. This includes initiatives such as flexible work arrangements, wellness programs, and promoting a culture that values work-life integration.*

4. **Developing Agile and Resilient Teams:** *With the pace of change accelerating,*

leaders prioritize building agile and resilient teams. They foster a growth mindset, encourage continuous learning, and promote adaptability among employees. Leaders empower their teams to embrace change, experiment, and learn from failures, enabling them to respond effectively to evolving challenges and seize opportunities.

5. **Enhancing Digital Transformation:** Leaders recognize the importance of embracing digital technologies and driving digital transformation within their organizations. They prioritize understanding emerging technologies, assessing their impact on the business, and leveraging them to improve processes, enhance customer experiences, and drive innovation.

6. **Strengthening Ethical Practices and Sustainability:** Leaders prioritize ethical decision-making and sustainable practices. They understand the significance of corporate social responsibility and incorporate ethical considerations into their strategic decisions. They champion sustainability initiatives, aligning business goals with environmental and social responsibility to create long-term value.

7. **Nurturing Leadership Development:** Leaders prioritize investing in the development of future leaders within their organizations. They identify and nurture talent, provide mentorship and coaching, and create opportunities for growth and advancement. Developing a strong leadership pipeline ensures the organization's long-term success and sustainability.

8. **Embracing Collaboration and Stakeholder Engagement:** Leaders recognize the importance of collaboration and stakeholder engagement. They foster strong relationships with customers, employees, shareholders, communities, and other stakeholders. By actively listening to diverse perspectives and involving stakeholders in decision-making processes, leaders can build trust, enhance innovation, and drive sustainable growth.

These new priorities reflect the evolving expectations placed on leaders to create purpose-driven, inclusive, and resilient organizations. By embracing these priorities, leaders can navigate complex challenges, inspire their teams, and drive meaningful change in today's rapidly changing business environment.

The best team leaders all have one thing in common:

They put leadership goals in place.

It's important for leaders to set goals for themselves so they can improve on the skillsets they already have. Setting specific, measurable, attainable, relevant, and time-based (SMART) goals can help leaders create an actionable plan to grow and succeed.

But with so much to do, entrepreneurs may stop seeing the value of personal learning and development. In reality, setting goals for your own leadership and management style can help you grow alongside your company.

To help you become the best leader you can be, we've compiled 15 leadership goals and objectives with SMART examples that every leader should aim for.

The following examples of leadership goals and objectives include ways to develop your professional and emotional well-being.

HOW CAN YOU MASTER OR FURTHER YOUR LEADERSHIP SKILLS

1. Become more adaptable to change.

Adaptability in the workplace *is more critical now than ever. Leaders must be prepared for every change in the business world. Especially so, they must be willing to adapt to the changing talent landscape amid the rise of* **remote work.**

*Today, talent desires **global mobility.** They want work-from-anywhere policies, a life-work balance, and flexible schedules. Great business leaders adjust their workforce model to serve the changing needs of today's talent in order to reap the long-term benefits of lower employee turnover, improved morale, and better business success.*

SMART goal example: Survey your team to understand the changes they want to see in the workplace, then make those changes where feasible. Maybe that means allowing employees to work from home or adjusting your employee rewards packages to include free access to mental health resources.

The following examples of leadership goals and objectives include ways to develop your professional and emotional well-being.

HOW CAN YOU MASTER OR FURTHER YOUR LEADERSHIP SKILLS

1. Become more adaptable to change.

Adaptability in the workplace *is more critical now than ever. Leaders must be prepared for every change in the business world. Especially so, they must be willing to adapt to the changing talent landscape amid the rise of **remote work**.*

*Today, talent desires **global mobility**. They want work-from-anywhere policies, a life-work balance, and flexible schedules. Great business leaders adjust their workforce model to serve the changing needs of today's talent in order to reap the long-term benefits of lower employee turnover, improved morale, and better business success.*

SMART goal example: Survey your team to understand the changes they want to see in the workplace, then make those changes where feasible. Maybe that means allowing employees to work from home or adjusting your employee rewards packages to include free access to mental health resources.

5. Learn to take constructive criticism.

Great leaders know how to take constructive criticism, which helps them become even better at their job. In a **study by LinkedIn,** 92% of people said that constructive criticism is effective at improving performance. When a leader is given upward feedback, specifically from their team, they can make tangible and relevant improvements to their workplace's day-to-day, boosting morale and performance.

SMART goal example: Increase the number of employees who provide upward feedback by 20%, showing your employees are comfortable doing so.

6. Practice confidence.

A little bit of confidence can inspire your team to follow you while helping you make smart decisions. Teams are more likely to follow confident leaders. But don't fret if you struggle to act or feel confident. You can work on building confidence by repeating mantras to yourself, making lists of your strong managerial qualities, and practicing mindfulness.

SMART goal example: Make a list of five of your strengths or work wins per week in a personal journal or digital document.

KEYS TO SETTING SUCCESSFUL GOALS

Setting successful goals involves careful planning and consideration. Here are key factors to keep in mind when setting goals:

1. ***Specificity****: Goals should be specific and clearly defined. Vague or general goals make it difficult to track progress and determine success. Define your goals with precision, including details such as what you want to achieve, why it is*

important, and any relevant metrics or deadlines.
2. **Measurability**: *Goals should be measurable, allowing you to track your progress and determine when you have achieved them. Establish clear criteria or metrics to assess your progress along the way. Measurable goals enable you to stay motivated and make adjustments if necessary.*
3. **Attainability**: *Goals should be challenging yet attainable. Consider your resources, skills, and capabilities when setting goals. Unrealistic or overly ambitious goals can lead to frustration and demotivation. Ensure that your goals are within reach while still pushing you out of your comfort zone.*
4. **Relevance**: *Goals should be relevant and aligned with your broader objectives, values, and priorities. Ensure that your goals are meaningful to you personally or to the organization you are part of. Aligning goals with your larger purpose increases motivation and commitment.*
5. **Time-bound:** *Goals should have a specific timeframe or deadline. Setting deadlines creates a sense of urgency and helps you stay focused and accountable. Break down long-term*

goals into shorter milestones to track progress and maintain momentum.
6. **Clarity and Communication:** Clearly communicate your goals to yourself and, when relevant, to others. Articulating your goals in writing or sharing them with a trusted friend, colleague, or mentor enhances commitment and accountability. Clarity in communication ensures everyone involved understands the objectives and can provide support or feedback.
7. **Flexibility and Adaptability:** Remain flexible and adaptable in the pursuit of your goals. Circumstances may change, requiring adjustments to your strategies or timelines. Being open to adapting your approach allows for continuous improvement and enables you to overcome obstacles more effectively.
8. **Action Planning and Tracking:** Break down your goals into actionable steps or tasks. Create a plan that outlines the specific actions you need to take to achieve your goals. Regularly track your progress, review your plan, and make adjustments as needed to stay on track.
9. **Motivation and Accountability:** Stay motivated by regularly reminding yourself of the reasons why you set the

goal. Find ways to keep your motivation high, such as by celebrating milestones or visualizing the desired outcome. Establish accountability mechanisms, whether through self-discipline, sharing progress with others, or seeking support from mentors or coaches.

10. ***Continuous Review and Learning:*** *Regularly review your goals to assess progress and make any necessary adjustments. Reflect on lessons learned, both from successes and setbacks, and integrate those insights into your future goal-setting process. Embrace a growth mindset, viewing setbacks as learning opportunities that can propel you forward.*

By following these key principles, you can set goals that are meaningful, actionable, and aligned with your aspirations, increasing the likelihood of success and personal fulfillment.

How to set (and achieve) personal goals in 8 steps

1. *Brainstorm your personal goals.*
2. *Visualize the future. ...*
3. *Break down your personal goals.*
4. *Make a list of your personal goals.*

5. *Set deadlines for your personal goals and schedule them.*
6. *Celebrate small wins.*
7. *Seek support. ...*
8. *Regularly review and adjust your personal goals.*

Certainly! **Here's a step-by-step guide to setting and achieving personal goals:**

1. **Brainstorm Your Personal Goals:** *Take some time to reflect on what you want to achieve in different areas of your life, such as career, relationships, health, personal development, and hobbies. Write down all the goals that come to mind without filtering them at this stage.*
2. **Visualize the Future**: *Imagine yourself in the future, having achieved your personal goals. Visualize how it looks, feels, and has an impact on your life. This exercise helps create a clear vision and motivates you to work towards your goals.*
3. **Break Down Your Personal Goals:** *Take each goal from your list and break it down into smaller, more manageable tasks or milestones. Breaking down goals into smaller steps makes them less*

overwhelming and allows for a clear action plan.
4. **Make a List of Your Personal Goals:** *Write down your personal goals in a specific and measurable format. Use the SMART framework: make them specific, measurable, achievable, relevant, and time-bound. This helps create clarity and sets a clear direction for your efforts.*
5. **Set Deadlines and Schedule Your Personal Goals:** *Assign deadlines to each of your goals and schedule them on your calendar or planner. By giving your goals a specific timeframe, you create a sense of urgency and commitment to take action.*
6. **Celebrate Small Wins:** *Acknowledge and celebrate your achievements along the way, even the small ones. Celebrating milestones boosts motivation and reinforces the belief that you're making progress towards your larger goals.*
7. **Seek support**: *Share your goals with trusted friends, family, or mentors who can support and encourage you throughout your journey. They can provide valuable insights, accountability, and motivation, especially during challenging times.*

8. ***Regularly review and adjust your personal goals.*** *Schedule regular check-ins to review your progress and make any necessary adjustments. Reflect on what's working well and what needs improvement. Be flexible and adapt your goals as circumstances change or new opportunities arise.*

By following these steps, you can set personal goals that are meaningful, actionable, and aligned with your aspirations. Remember to stay committed, stay focused, and stay motivated as you work towards achieving your goals.

PARETO PRINCIPLE

The Pareto Principle, also known as the 80/20 rule or the law of the vital few, states that roughly 80% of the effects come from 20% of the causes. This principle is based on the observation made by Italian economist Vilfredo Pareto, who noticed that approximately 80% of the land in Italy was owned by 20% of the population.

The Pareto Principle has been widely applied in various fields, including business, economics, time management, and productivity. It suggests that a small portion of input or effort often leads to a large portion of the results or outcomes. Here's a breakdown of the key aspects of the Pareto Principle:

1. **Imbalance of Cause and Effect:** The Pareto Principle highlights the imbalance between inputs and outputs. It suggests that not all causes or efforts contribute equally to the desired outcomes. Instead, a small percentage of causes or efforts have a significant impact, while the majority have a relatively lesser effect.

2. **Focus on the Vital Few**: The principle emphasizes the importance of identifying and focusing on the vital few factors that yield the majority of the results. By identifying and prioritizing these crucial factors, individuals and organizations can optimize their efforts and resources for maximum impact.

3. **Decision-Making and Resource Allocation:** The Pareto Principle can guide decision-making and resource allocation. It suggests that by identifying the 20% of causes or efforts

that generate 80% of the results, individuals and organizations can allocate their time, energy, and resources more effectively to achieve desired outcomes.

4. **Time Management and Productivity:** Applying the Pareto Principle to time management suggests that roughly 20% of our activities or tasks contribute to 80% of our productivity or desired outcomes. By identifying and prioritizing the most impactful activities, individuals can optimize their time and productivity.

5. **Continuous Improvement:** The Pareto Principle can be used to identify areas for improvement. By analyzing data or feedback, individuals or organizations can identify the few critical issues that are causing the majority of problems or inefficiencies. By addressing these vital issues, significant improvements can be achieved.

It's important to note that the 80/20 split is not always exact and can vary. The purpose of the Pareto Principle is to highlight the concept of disproportionate impact and encourage individuals and organizations to identify and focus on the most influential factors or efforts.

By understanding and applying the Pareto Principle, individuals and organizations can prioritize their efforts, allocate resources effectively, and achieve higher levels of efficiency and productivity.

How do you apply the Pareto principle to a business?

Applying the Pareto Principle to a business involves identifying and focusing on the key areas that generate the most significant impact on results. Here's how you can apply the Pareto Principle in a business context:

1. ***Identify High-Impact Factors**: Analyze your business data, such as sales, customers, products, or processes, to identify the factors that contribute the most to your desired outcomes. This could include the top-selling products, the most profitable customers, or key drivers of customer satisfaction. Look for patterns or trends that highlight the vital few factors that generate the majority of your business results.*
2. ***Prioritize Resources:** Once you have identified the high-impact factors, allocate your resources, including time, budget, and personnel, to focus on those*

areas. Devote more attention, effort, and resources to the vital few factors that generate the most significant results. This ensures that you optimize your resources for maximum impact and avoid spreading them too thin across less impactful areas.

3. **Optimize Marketing and Sales Strategies:** Apply the Pareto Principle to your marketing and sales efforts. Identify the customer segments or channels that generate the majority of your revenue or profits. Focus your marketing campaigns, sales efforts, and resources on those segments or channels to maximize your returns. This helps you prioritize your marketing and sales activities to reach the most valuable customers or prospects.

4. **Streamline Product or Service Offerings:** Analyze your product or service portfolio to identify the most profitable or in-demand offerings. Focus on optimizing those offerings further, investing in their development, marketing, and customer support. Consider streamlining or eliminating less profitable or low-demand offerings that consume resources without significant returns.

5. ***Customer Relationship Management:*** *Apply the Pareto Principle to your customer relationships. Identify the key customers who contribute the most to your business's revenue or loyalty. Provide them with personalized attention, excellent service, and targeted offers to maintain and strengthen those relationships. Understand their needs and preferences to ensure you deliver the most value to your most important customers.*

6. ***Continuous Improvement:*** *Continuously analyze your business data and performance metrics to identify areas for improvement. Apply the Pareto Principle to find the few critical issues or bottlenecks that are causing the majority of problems or inefficiencies. Focus your improvement efforts on addressing those vital issues to yield significant overall improvements.*

7. ***Time and Task Management:*** *Apply the Pareto Principle to your own time and task management. Identify the tasks or activities that contribute the most to your productivity or business results. Prioritize those tasks and allocate your time and energy accordingly. Delegate or eliminate low-impact or non-essential*

tasks to free up time for high-impact activities.

Remember that the application of the Pareto Principle will vary depending on your specific industry, business model, and goals. Regular data analysis, performance tracking, and strategic decision-making are crucial to effectively applying the Pareto Principle in your business and driving meaningful results.

GTD METHODOLOGY

The GTD (Getting Things Done) methodology, developed by productivity consultant David Allen, is a widely recognized approach to personal and professional productivity. GTD provides a systematic framework for organizing and managing tasks, projects, and information. Its core principles focus on capturing, clarifying, organizing, reflecting, and engaging with tasks and commitments. Here's an overview of the GTD methodology:

1. ***Capture**: The first step in GTD is to capture all your tasks, ideas, commitments, and any other open loops that are on your mind. This involves collecting everything into a trusted system or inbox, whether it's physical or digital. By capturing all your "stuff" in one place, you free your mind from trying to remember everything.*
2. ***Clarify**: Once you have captured everything, go through each item one by one and clarify what it means and what needs to be done. Ask yourself, "What is the next action required to move this forward?" If an item requires multiple steps, break it down into actionable tasks. If it takes less than two minutes to complete, David Allen suggests doing it immediately.*
3. ***Organize**: After clarifying your tasks, organize them into appropriate categories or lists. The main lists in GTD include Next Actions (tasks that can be*

done right away), Projects (multi-step outcomes), Waiting For (tasks waiting for someone else's input), Someday/Maybe (ideas or tasks you may want to do in the future), and Reference (information you need to keep for reference).

4. **Reflect**: *Regularly review and reflect on your lists and commitments. Conduct weekly and monthly reviews to ensure that you are aware of all your tasks and commitments and that your system is up-to-date. Use this time to reassess priorities, make adjustments, and identify any new tasks or projects that need to be captured and clarified.*

5. **Engage**: *Once you have a clear view of your tasks and commitments, decide what to do and take action. GTD encourages a "do it, delegate it, defer it, or drop it" approach. If a task can be done quickly, do it right away. If it requires someone else's attention, delegate it. If it can't be done immediately, defer it by scheduling it or adding it to your Next Actions list. If a task is no longer relevant or necessary, drop it.*

The GTD methodology emphasizes the importance of maintaining a trusted external system to capture, clarify, and organize tasks and commitments. By having a comprehensive system in place, you can free up mental space, reduce stress, and increase productivity by focusing on what needs to be done at any given moment.

It's worth noting that while GTD provides a framework, the specific tools and techniques used to implement it can vary from person to person. Many individuals use digital tools, such as task management apps or software, to implement the GTD methodology effectively.

What is the GDT method?

The Getting Things Done method revolves around five simple steps to help you manage tasks effectively.

1. *Capture. Capture everything that has got your attention into a trusted external system like a piece of paper or your to-do list app.*
2. *Clarify. ...*
3. *Organize. ...*
4. *Reflect. ...*
5. *Engage.*

What is GDT's importance?

GD&T gives manufacturers a clear understanding of the tolerances for a specific part. It provides the maximum amount of tolerance for the part to function properly, which reduces part complexity so that you aren't overspending for a minimum tolerance that you may not need.

PROCRASTINATION

Procrastination refers to the act of delaying or postponing tasks or actions, often resulting in a later start or completion time than originally intended. It involves putting off important or *necessary activities in favor of more immediate and less important tasks, distractions, or even doing nothing at all. Procrastination can have negative consequences for productivity, efficiency, and overall well-being. Here are some key aspects to understand about procrastination:*

1. ***Causes and Triggers:*** *Procrastination can stem from various factors, including fear of failure, perfectionism, lack of motivation, feeling overwhelmed, unclear goals, or difficulty prioritizing tasks. It can also be triggered by external factors such as distractions, a lack of structure or accountability, or a habit of delaying tasks.*
2. ***Short-Term Gratification:*** *Procrastination often occurs because individuals seek immediate gratification or relief from discomfort by engaging in more enjoyable or less demanding activities. This could involve checking social media, watching videos, or engaging in other forms of entertainment instead of addressing important tasks.*
3. ***Negative Impact:*** *Procrastination can have several negative consequences. It can result in increased stress and*

anxiety as unfinished tasks accumulate. It may lead to missed deadlines, compromised quality of work, lower productivity, and a negative impact on personal and professional reputation. Procrastination can also hinder personal growth, delay progress towards goals, and limit overall success.

4. **Overcoming Procrastination:** Overcoming procrastination requires self-awareness, discipline, and proactive strategies. Here are some techniques that can help.
5. **Set clear goals and prioritize:** Clearly define your goals and break them down into smaller, actionable tasks. Prioritize tasks based on importance and urgency.
6. **Create a plan and schedule.** Develop a detailed plan for each task and allocate specific time slots to work on them. Use calendars, to-do lists, or task management tools to schedule and track your progress.
7. **Manage Distractions:** Identify and minimize distractions that contribute to procrastination. This may involve turning off notifications, creating a dedicated workspace, or using website blockers to limit access to time-wasting websites.

8. ***Develop Accountability:*** *Share your goals and progress with others who can hold you accountable. This could be a friend, colleague, or mentor who can provide support, encouragement, and check-ins.*
9. ***Break Tasks Into Smaller Steps****: If a task seems overwhelming, break it down into smaller, manageable steps. This makes it easier to get started and build momentum.*
10. ***Utilize Time Management Techniques:*** *Explore time management techniques such as the Pomodoro Technique (working in focused bursts with timed breaks) or time blocking (allocating specific time periods for different tasks)*
11. ***Address Underlying Issues:*** *Reflect on any underlying factors contributing to procrastination, such as fear of failure or perfectionism. Challenge negative beliefs and seek support or professional help if needed.*

Overcoming procrastination is a process that requires consistent effort and self-discipline. By understanding the causes and implementing effective strategies, individuals can develop better habits, improve productivity, and accomplish their goals more efficiently.

Is procrastination the same as being lazy?

Procrastination is often confused with laziness, but they are very different.

*Procrastination is an **active** process; you **choose** to do something else instead of the task that you know you should be doing. In contrast, laziness suggests apathy, inactivity, and an unwillingness to act.*

Procrastination usually involves ignoring an unpleasant, but likely more important, task in favor of one that is more enjoyable or easier.

But giving in to this impulse can have serious consequences. For example, even minor episodes of procrastination can make us feel guilty or ashamed. It can lead to reduced productivity and cause us to miss out on achieving our goals.

If we procrastinate over a long period of time, we can become demotivated and disillusioned with our work, which can lead to depression and even job loss in extreme cases.

Top 5 Tips to Stop Procrastination

1. **Start small.** Break large tasks into smaller chunks, and pick one that you can do **now**—so that you're underway almost without realizing it!
2. **Make a plan.** Put times or dates on the key tasks on your list so that you know what to concentrate on and when.
3. **Finish things.** When you spot a task that's nearly done, put extra effort into getting it over the line. Don't be tempted to leave lots of jobs **almost** finished; enjoy the satisfaction of ticking them off your list!
4. **Deal with distractions.** What can you change about your environment to improve your focus? What needs to be put out of reach until this task is done?
5. **Be kind to yourself.** No one ever gets to the end of their to-do list! Do your best to meet your deadlines and celebrate your successes. But be realistic: you'll always have more to do than there are hours in the day.

How to Overcome Procrastination

As with most habits, it is possible to overcome procrastination. Follow the steps below to help you deal with and prevent procrastination:

Step 1: Recognize That You're Procrastinating

You might be putting off a task because you've had to re-prioritize your workload. If you're briefly delaying an important task for a genuinely good reason, then you aren't necessarily procrastinating. However, if you start to put things off indefinitely or switch focus because you want to avoid doing something, then you probably are.

You may also be procrastinating if you:

- *Fill your day with low-priority tasks.*
- *Leave an item on your to-do list for a long time, even though it's important.*
- *Read emails several times over without making a decision on what to do with them.*
- *Start a high-priority task and then go off to make coffee.*
- *Fill your time with unimportant tasks that other people ask you to do instead of getting on with the important tasks already on your list.*

- *Wait to be in the "right mood" or wait for the "right time" to tackle a task.*

EFFECTIVE MEETINGS, MEETINGS WITH ACTION

Effective meetings, also known as meetings with action, are meetings that are purposeful, well-organized, and result-oriented. These meetings aim to maximize productivity, engagement, and outcomes by ensuring that clear objectives are set, relevant participants are involved, and specific actions are identified and assigned. Here are some key elements of effective meetings:

1. ***Clear Objectives:*** *Every effective meeting should have a clear purpose and well-defined objectives. The meeting organizer should determine what they want to achieve through the meeting and communicate those objectives to the participants in advance. This helps focus the discussion and guide decision-making.*
2. ***Thoughtful Planning****: Effective meetings require thoughtful planning and preparation. The organizer should create an agenda that outlines the topics to be covered, the time allocated*

for each item, and any necessary materials or resources. Sharing the agenda with participants beforehand allows them to come prepared and contribute meaningfully.
3. **Relevant Participants:** To ensure effectiveness, invite only the key stakeholders and individuals who have a direct impact on or contribute to the meeting's objectives. Having the right people in the room helps facilitate productive discussions and decision-making. Consider whether all participants need to be physically present or if remote participation is feasible.
4. **Time Management:** Time management is crucial to maintaining the effectiveness of a meeting. Start and end the meeting on time, and adhere to the allocated time for each agenda item. The meeting organizer should guide the discussion and prevent tangents or unrelated discussions that can derail the meeting's focus.
5. **Engaging Communication:** Encourage active participation and engagement from all attendees. Create an environment where everyone feels comfortable sharing their ideas, asking

questions, and providing input. The meeting organizer can use facilitation techniques, such as round-robin discussions or brainstorming exercises, to promote interaction and collaboration.

6. **Action-Oriented:** Effective meetings result in action and progress. During the meeting, decisions should be made, tasks or action items should be assigned, and deadlines should be established. Clearly document the action items, responsible parties, and due dates. This ensures that the discussions and decisions translate into tangible outcomes.

7. **Follow-Up and Accountability:** After the meeting, the organizer should distribute meeting minutes or a summary that includes a recap of decisions made, action items assigned, and any relevant notes. This serves as a reference for participants and ensures clarity and accountability. Regularly follow up on action items and track progress to ensure they are being completed.

8. **Continuous Improvement:** Effective meetings should be part of an ongoing process of improvement. Encourage

participants to provide feedback on meeting effectiveness, structure, and content. Use this feedback to refine future meetings and make them more efficient and valuable.

By implementing these elements, meetings can become more purposeful, action-oriented, and productive. Effective meetings respect participants' time, achieve desired outcomes, and contribute to overall organizational success.

What is an effective meeting?

Effective meetings have high participation, good energy, constructive collaboration, and meaningful conversations. In short, effective meetings are those that tap into the wisdom, expertise, and energy of the group. Effective meetings are interactive and valuable to both the meeting leader and the meeting attendees.

Running a successful meeting involves careful planning, effective facilitation, and a focus on achieving desired outcomes.

Here are key steps to help you run a successful meeting:

1. **Set a Clear Agenda:** Start by creating a clear and concise agenda that outlines the topics to be discussed and the objectives of the meeting. Share the agenda with participants in advance so they can come prepared.
2. **Know Your Desired Outcomes:** Clearly define the desired outcomes or goals you want to achieve through the meeting. This helps keep the discussion focused and ensures everyone is working towards a common purpose.
3. **Find the Right Environment:** Choose a suitable meeting space that allows for comfortable seating, good visibility, and minimal distractions. Ensure the necessary audiovisual equipment or technology is available and functioning properly.
4. **Prepare Talking Points:** Prepare talking points or key discussion items for each agenda item. This will help guide the flow of the meeting and ensure important topics are addressed. Share the talking points with participants so they can contribute effectively.
5. **Give Everyone a Chance to Speak:** Encourage active participation and ensure everyone has an opportunity to contribute their thoughts and

perspectives. Facilitate open and respectful discussions, allowing different viewpoints to be heard and considered.

6. **Encourage Ideas and Solutions:** *Foster a collaborative and creative environment where participants feel comfortable sharing their ideas and suggestions. Encourage brainstorming and problem-solving discussions to generate innovative solutions.*
7. **Be Mindful of the Time**: *Time management is crucial for a successful meeting. Start and end the meeting on time, and allocate appropriate time for each agenda item. Be mindful of the discussion's pace and steer the conversation to stay on track.*
8. **Define clear next steps and actions:** *Summarize key decisions, action items, and responsibilities at the end of the meeting. Clearly communicate the next steps and deadlines, ensuring everyone understands their roles and tasks. Follow up with meeting minutes or a summary to document the outcomes.*
9. **Facilitate Effective Communication**: *As the meeting leader, facilitate effective communication by actively listening, paraphrasing key points, and asking clarifying questions. Ensure that*

everyone's input is valued, and encourage constructive dialogue.

10. ***Evaluate and continuously improve:*** *After the meeting, reflect on its effectiveness and seek feedback from participants. Identify areas for improvement and make adjustments for future meetings. Continuous improvement ensures that meetings become more productive and meaningful over time.*

By following these steps, you can create a productive and efficient meeting environment that encourages active participation, drives decision-making, and achieves desired outcomes.

PRODUCTIVITY OR PRESENTEEISM?

Productivity and presenteeism are two concepts related to work performance, but they have distinct meanings:

1. ***Productivity****: Productivity refers to the measure of output or work accomplished in relation to the resources, such as time,*

effort, or materials, invested. It focuses on the efficiency and effectiveness of work. A productive individual or organization consistently achieves desired results in a timely manner while optimizing resources.

Factors that can enhance productivity include effective time management, prioritization, goal setting, focus, skill development, collaboration, and leveraging tools and technologies. Improving productivity often involves streamlining processes, eliminating unnecessary tasks, and optimizing workflows.

2. **Presenteeism**: *Presenteeism, on the other hand, refers to the phenomenon where employees are physically present at work but are not fully engaged or productive. It occurs when individuals show up for work despite being unwell, fatigued, or facing personal issues that affect their ability to perform at their best.*

Presenteeism can result from various factors, such as a fear of negative consequences for taking time off, heavy workloads, poor work-life balance, a lack of job satisfaction, or a culture that values long hours over actual productivity. While physically present, employees may exhibit reduced concentration, lower motivation, decreased creativity, and decreased efficiency, leading to subpar performance and diminished contributions.

It's important to note that presenteeism can have negative consequences for both individual employees and organizations. It can lead to decreased job satisfaction, increased stress levels, burnout, and higher rates of errors and accidents. Moreover, it can negatively impact team morale and overall productivity.

Organizations can address presenteeism by fostering a supportive work environment that encourages work-life balance, promotes employee well-being, offers flexibility, and values open communication. Encouraging employees to take appropriate time off when needed and providing resources for managing personal challenges are key steps to mitigate presenteeism.

In summary, productivity focuses on achieving optimal output and results, while presenteeism refers to being physically present but not fully engaged or productive. Prioritizing productivity and addressing presenteeism can contribute to a healthier and more efficient work environment.

What is the productivity of an employee?

What is employee productivity? Employee productivity is generally understood as the ability of an employee to take input (instructions, directions, requirements, etc.) and turn it into output. Effectively, it's the measure of how employees produce input and turn it into output in a given period of time.

The productivity of an employee refers to their ability to generate output or complete tasks efficiently and effectively within a given period of time. It is a measure of how much value or work an employee contributes to the organization. Employee productivity is influenced by various factors, including skills, knowledge, motivation, the work environment, and available resources.

Here are a few key aspects of employee productivity:

1. **Output**: *Employee productivity is often measured by the quantity or quality of work completed. It can be assessed based on tangible deliverables, such as completed projects, sales targets*

achieved, customer satisfaction ratings, or other relevant performance metrics specific to the employee's role.
2. **Efficiency:** Productivity also considers the efficiency with which work is performed. This includes the ability to complete tasks in a timely manner, minimize waste or rework, optimize processes, and utilize resources effectively. Efficient employees accomplish their work with fewer errors, interruptions, or unnecessary delays.
3. **Time Management:** Effective time management is crucial for employee productivity. It involves prioritizing tasks, setting goals, organizing work schedules, and balancing competing demands. Employees who can allocate their time wisely and focus on high-priority activities tend to be more productive.
4. **Skills and Knowledge:** Employee productivity is influenced by the skills, expertise, and knowledge they possess. Continuous learning, professional development, and staying up-to-date with industry trends can enhance employee productivity by enabling them to perform tasks more effectively and efficiently.

5. ***Motivation and Engagement:*** *The level of motivation and engagement an employee experiences significantly impacts their productivity. When employees are motivated, they exhibit higher levels of commitment, initiative, and enthusiasm towards their work. Organizations can foster motivation by providing recognition, challenging assignments, opportunities for growth, and a supportive work environment.*
6. ***Collaboration and Communication:*** *Productivity can be enhanced through effective collaboration and communication. Employees who actively engage with their colleagues, share knowledge, seek feedback, and participate in teamwork can achieve better results by leveraging collective expertise and resources.*
7. ***Work-Life Balance**: Employee productivity can be influenced by their ability to achieve a healthy work-life balance. Encouraging employees to maintain a balance between work responsibilities and personal well-being helps prevent burnout, improves focus, and promotes overall productivity.*

It's important to note that productivity is not solely the responsibility of individual employees. Creating a supportive work culture, providing adequate resources, clear expectations, and providing leadership support are crucial for fostering employee productivity.

Organizations strive to enhance employee productivity, as it directly impacts their overall performance, efficiency, and competitiveness. By understanding the factors that contribute to productivity, organizations can implement strategies to optimize employee performance and create an environment that supports high levels of productivity.

Employee productivity can be measured in various ways, depending on the nature of work and available data. Here are a few common methods used to measure employee productivity:

1. ***Output-Based Metrics***: *This approach measures productivity by focusing on the output or results achieved by an employee. It looks at specific deliverables, such as completed tasks, projects, sales targets, customer satisfaction ratings, or revenue*

generated. Output-based metrics provide a clear indicator of the employee's contribution to the organization's goals.
2. **Efficiency Metrics:** Efficiency metrics assess the productivity of employees by considering the time, effort, or resources used to accomplish tasks. These metrics may include measures such as the time taken to complete a task, the number of units produced per hour, or the cost-effectiveness of the employee's work.
3. **3. Key Performance Indicators (KPIs):** KPIs are specific metrics that align with organizational goals and objectives. They can be used to measure employee productivity by focusing on critical areas of performance. Examples of KPIs include sales targets, customer retention rates, error rates, response times, or production quotas.
4. **Time-Based Metrics:** Some industries or roles rely on time-based metrics to measure productivity. This involves tracking the number of hours worked or specific time spent on different activities. For example, in industries where billable hours are important, tracking the amount of time spent on

client work can provide insights into employee productivity.
5. **Employee Feedback and Evaluations:** Gathering feedback from supervisors, colleagues, or customers can provide qualitative insights into an employee's productivity. Performance evaluations, self-assessments, or 360-degree feedback processes can help assess an employee's effectiveness, collaboration skills, and contribution to the team or organization.
6. **Comparative Analysis**: Comparing an employee's performance to that of their peers or industry benchmarks can be useful in measuring productivity. This approach involves analyzing how an employee's output, efficiency, or performance measures up against similar roles or industry standards.
7. **Technological Tools and Data Analysis:** With the increasing use of technology in the workplace, various tools and software applications can help measure employee productivity. These tools can track task completion, time spent on specific activities, or provide data on work patterns and trends.

It's important to note that measuring employee productivity should be done with care and consideration. Productivity metrics should align with the organization's goals, be relevant to the specific role, and take into account the unique aspects of the work being performed. Additionally, it's essential to consider the quality of work, employee well-being, and other factors that contribute to overall performance.

Ultimately, a combination of quantitative and qualitative methods, tailored to the specific context, can provide a comprehensive understanding of employee productivity. Regular monitoring and evaluation, coupled with effective feedback and support, can help drive continuous improvement and optimize employee performance.

HOW CAN YOU MASTER OR FURTHER YOUR LEADERSHIP SKILLS

SECTION FOUR :

TEAM LEADERSHIP

HIGH-PERFORMANCE TEAM

KEYS TO OPTIMIZE YOUR LEADERSHIP STYLE

MOTIVATING AND EFFECTIVE PERFORMANCE APPRAISAL

COMMITMENT, MOTIVATION AND TALENT RETENTION

HOW TO MANAGE RESISTANCE TO CHANGE SUCCESSFULLY

GENERATIONAL CLASH: MILLENNIALS TELEWORK AND VIRTUAL TEAMS

HIGH-PERFORMANCE TEAM

A high-performance team is a group of individuals who work collaboratively to achieve exceptional results and exceed expectations. Such teams are characterized by their ability to consistently deliver outstanding outcomes, demonstrate exceptional productivity, and exhibit a high level of synergy and cohesion.

Here are some key characteristics and principles of a high-performing team:

1. **Clear goals and shared vision:** *The team has a well-defined purpose and specific goals that are understood and embraced by all members. They share a common vision, which provides them with a sense of direction and motivation.*
2. **Complementary skills and roles:** *high-performance teams consist of members with diverse skill sets and expertise that complement each other. Each team member has a clearly defined role and responsibilities that align with their*

strengths and contribute to the overall success of the team.
3. **Trust and psychological safety**: Trust is a crucial element within high-performance teams. Members trust and rely on one another, creating an environment of psychological safety where individuals feel comfortable expressing their ideas, taking risks, and being vulnerable without fear of judgment or reprisal.
4. **Effective communication**: open and transparent communication is vital for high-performance teams. They foster an environment where team members actively listen, share information, provide constructive feedback, and ensure everyone is on the same page. Clear communication channels and regular updates are established to facilitate information flow.
5. **Collaboration and synergy:** High-performance teams value collaboration and leverage the collective intelligence of their members. They encourage cooperation, synergy, and the exchange of ideas to achieve optimal outcomes. Team members support each other, share knowledge, and work together to

solve problems and make informed decisions.
6. **Accountability and ownership:** Each member of a high-performance team takes responsibility for their actions and outcomes. They hold themselves and others accountable, ensuring that deadlines are met, commitments are honored, and quality standards are maintained. Performance is regularly evaluated, and feedback is provided to foster continuous improvement.
7. **Adaptability and resilience:** high-performance teams are adaptable and resilient in the face of challenges and changes. They embrace innovation and are open to new ideas, allowing them to respond effectively to evolving circumstances and seize opportunities for growth.
8. **Continuous learning and improvement:** These teams have a culture of continuous learning and improvement. They encourage individual and collective development, seek feedback, and actively reflect on their performance. Lessons learned from both successes and failures are used to refine processes and enhance future performance.

Overall, high-performance teams are characterized by a collective commitment to excellence, a supportive and empowering environment, and a focus on achieving exceptional results through collaboration, communication, and continuous improvement.

Certainly! Here are some key characteristics of high-performing teams:

1. **Clear and Aligned Goals:** *High-performing teams have a shared understanding of their goals and objectives. They know what they are working towards and why it matters. The team members are aligned and committed to achieving these goals.*
2. **Trust and Psychological Safety:** *Trust is the foundation of high-performing teams. Team members trust and rely on each other's capabilities, judgments, and intentions. There is a sense of psychological safety, allowing individuals to take risks, share ideas, and express their opinions without fear of negative consequences.*
3. **Effective Communication:** *High-performing teams have open and transparent communication channels. Team members actively listen to each*

other, provide constructive feedback, and share relevant information in a timely manner. They communicate clearly, ensuring that everyone understands expectations and stays informed.

4. ***Complementary Skills and Roles:*** *High-performing teams consist of individuals with diverse skills and expertise. Each team member brings something unique to the table, and their roles are clearly defined and complementary. The team leverages these skills to accomplish tasks efficiently and effectively.*

5. ***Collaboration and Synergy:*** *Collaboration is a hallmark of high-performing teams. They work together, leveraging each other's strengths and knowledge to achieve shared goals. The team members engage in active problem-solving, idea sharing, and decision-making, leading to synergistic outcomes.*

6. ***Accountability and Ownership:*** *High-performing teams foster a culture of accountability. Each team member takes responsibility for their actions, deliverables, and outcomes. They hold themselves and others accountable,*

ensuring that commitments are honored and deadlines are met.
7. **Continuous Learning and Improvement:** High-performing teams are committed to ongoing learning and improvement. They actively seek feedback, reflect on their performance, and apply lessons learned from both successes and failures. This mindset of continuous improvement drives innovation and growth.
8. **Adaptability and Resilience:** High-performing teams are flexible and adaptable in the face of challenges and change. They embrace new ideas, remain agile, and adjust their strategies as needed. They are resilient, bouncing back from setbacks and maintaining a positive mindset.
9. **Supportive Team Culture:** High-performing teams foster a supportive and inclusive team culture. They celebrate each other's successes, provide support during difficult times, and promote a sense of belonging. The team members care for each other, creating a positive work environment that enhances collaboration and productivity.

10. ***Results-Oriented***: High-performing teams are focused on achieving results. They have a strong work ethic, prioritize tasks effectively, and consistently deliver high-quality outcomes. They set high standards, monitor progress, and celebrate their achievements.

These characteristics collectively contribute to the success of high-performing teams, allowing them to excel in their performance and achieve outstanding results.for example, with the diagram below.

Examples of high-performing teams

- Project teams. ...
- Management teams. ...
- Virtual teams. ...
- Autonomous work teams. ...
- Trust between team members. ...
- Complementary skill sets. ...
- Well-defined roles. ...
- Good communication.

What are the four qualities of high-performance teams?

There are several different models and frameworks that outline the qualities of high-performance teams. One popular model, *developed by Jon R. Katzenbach and Douglas K. Smith, identifies four core qualities of high-performance teams. These qualities are:*

1. **Common Purpose**: *High-performance teams have a shared sense of purpose and a clear understanding of their mission and goals. They are aligned around a common objective and are committed to achieving it. The common purpose provides focus and direction, helping the team members prioritize their efforts and work together towards a common goal.*
2. **Clear Roles and Responsibilities**: *Each member of a high-performance team has a clearly defined role and set of responsibilities that align with their skills and expertise. Clear roles help avoid confusion and duplication of efforts while ensuring that each team member understands their contribution to the team's success. When everyone understands their roles, they can work together more effectively and efficiently.*
3. **Effective Communication**: *Effective communication is crucial for high-performance teams. It involves active listening, open and honest dialogue, and the ability to express ideas and concerns*

freely. High-performance teams create an environment where communication flows freely, feedback is given constructively, and information is shared transparently. This enables better collaboration, coordination, and decision-making within the team.

4. ***Mutual Accountability:*** *Mutual accountability means that each team member is responsible for their own performance and the collective performance of the team. High-performance teams hold themselves and each other accountable for delivering on commitments, meeting deadlines, and achieving shared goals. They establish a culture of trust and respect where individuals feel comfortable holding others accountable for their contributions.*

These four qualities—common purpose, clear roles and responsibilities, effective communication, and mutual accountability—work together to create a strong foundation for high-performance teams. By embodying these qualities, teams can enhance their collaboration, productivity, and overall effectiveness in achieving exceptional results.

Developing a high-performing team requires intentional effort and focus from managers and team leaders.

Here's a breakdown of key areas and strategies to develop a high-performing team:

1. ***Prioritize Communication****: Effective communication is crucial for building a high-performing team. Encourage open and transparent communication channels where team members feel comfortable sharing ideas, concerns, and feedback. Foster active listening and provide opportunities for everyone to contribute to discussions.*
2. ***Set SMART Objectives****: Clearly define and communicate specific, measurable, achievable, relevant, and time-bound (SMART) objectives for the team. This provides clarity and focus, ensuring that everyone understands what needs to be accomplished and how success will be measured.*
3. ***Tackle Conflict****: Conflict within a team can hinder performance. Encourage a culture where conflicts are addressed openly and constructively. Provide conflict resolution techniques, promote*

understanding, and facilitate healthy discussions to find mutually beneficial solutions. Addressing conflicts promptly can strengthen relationships and improve team dynamics.
4. **Understand Current and Future Dynamics:** Gain a deep understanding of the current dynamics within the team, including individual strengths, weaknesses, and working styles. Use this information to create diverse and complementary teams and to assign roles that align with individuals' skills and interests. Also, consider the future dynamics and skill requirements to ensure the team is adaptable and prepared for upcoming challenges.
5. **Master Emotional Intelligence:** Emotional intelligence (EI) plays a significant role in team dynamics and performance. Develop EI skills within team members and leaders to enhance self-awareness, empathy, and effective communication. Encourage a supportive environment where emotions are acknowledged and managed constructively.
6. **Establish Trust:** Trust is the foundation of high-performing teams. Encourage trust-building activities, promote

transparency, and lead by example. Foster an environment where team members feel safe to take risks, share ideas, and express concerns without fear of judgment or negative consequences. Trust enables collaboration, innovation, and increased productivity.
7. **Feedback is a gift.** *Establish a culture of continuous feedback and growth. Provide regular feedback to team members, recognizing their achievements and addressing areas for improvement. Encourage peer-to-peer feedback and create opportunities for self-reflection and personal development. Emphasize the importance of learning from both successes and failures.*

By focusing on these areas, managers can create an environment that nurtures a high-performing team. It requires ongoing attention, support, and an investment in the development of individuals and the team as a whole.

KEYS TO OPTIMIZE YOUR LEADERSHIP STYLE

Optimizing your leadership style involves refining and enhancing your approach to effectively lead and inspire your team. Here are some key principles and strategies to consider:

1. ***Self-awareness****: Develop a deep understanding of your strengths, weaknesses, values, and leadership style. Reflect on your leadership behaviors and how they impact others. Recognize areas for improvement and*

be open to feedback. Self-awareness allows you to align your actions with your values and make conscious choices as a leader.
2. **Adaptability**: Recognize that different situations and individuals may require different leadership approaches. Be flexible and adaptable in your leadership style, adjusting your strategies to meet the needs of your team members and the evolving circumstances. This includes being open to new ideas and perspectives and being willing to change course when necessary.
3. **Effective Communication:** Communication is a fundamental aspect of leadership. Develop strong communication skills, including active listening, clear and concise messaging, and the ability to convey information effectively to diverse audiences. Tailor your communication style to each individual and situation, ensuring that your messages are understood and inspiring.
4. **Empowering and Delegating:** Foster a culture of empowerment and delegate tasks and responsibilities to team members. Trust their capabilities and

provide them with the autonomy to make decisions and take ownership of their work. This not only builds their confidence but also allows you to focus on strategic priorities and leverage the expertise of your team.

5. **Building Relationships and Trust:** *Invest time in building relationships with your team members. Get to know them on a personal level, show genuine interest in their well-being, and create a supportive and inclusive environment. Build trust through transparency, integrity, and consistency in your actions. Trust is essential for collaboration, open communication, and high performance.*

6. **Continuous Learning and Development:** *Commit to ongoing personal and professional development. Stay up-to-date with industry trends, leadership theories, and best practices. Seek opportunities to expand your knowledge and skills through training, workshops, reading, and networking. Encourage a culture of learning within your team, supporting the growth and development of your team members as well.*

7. ***Leading by Example:*** *Demonstrate the behaviors and values you expect from your team. Lead by example in terms of work ethic, integrity, accountability, and professionalism. Model the behaviors you want to see in your team members and inspire them through your actions. Be authentic and consistent in your leadership approach.*
8. ***Emotional Intelligence:*** *Develop emotional intelligence, which involves understanding and managing your emotions and those of others. Cultivate empathy, self-awareness, and the ability to recognize and regulate emotions in yourself and others. This allows you to connect with your team on a deeper level, understand their needs, and respond empathetically.*

By focusing on these key aspects, you can optimize your leadership style and create an environment where your team members thrive, collaborate effectively, and achieve exceptional results. Remember that leadership is an ongoing journey of growth and improvement, and it requires continuous reflection and refinement.

Certainly! Here are ten tips for improving leadership skills:

1. ***Seek Feedback:*** *Actively seek feedback from your team members, colleagues, and mentors. Listen to their perspectives, learn from their insights, and use the feedback to identify areas for improvement. Embrace feedback as an opportunity to grow and refine your leadership approach.*
2. ***Continuously Learn:*** *Commit to lifelong learning. Stay updated on industry trends, leadership theories, and best practices. Read books, attend seminars or webinars, and pursue professional development opportunities. Expand your knowledge and skills to enhance your leadership capabilities.*
3. ***Develop emotional intelligence.*** *Emotional intelligence is crucial for effective leadership. Foster self-awareness, empathy, and the ability to understand and manage emotions in yourself and others. Cultivate strong interpersonal skills and build positive relationships with your team members.*
4. ***Communicate Effectively:*** *Develop strong communication skills. Clearly articulate your vision, expectations, and*

goals. Listen actively to others, encourage open dialogue, and provide constructive feedback. Tailor your communication style to different audiences and be a proficient and persuasive communicator.

5. **Delegate and Empower:** Delegate tasks and responsibilities to your team members. Trust their capabilities and provide them with the autonomy to make decisions and take ownership of their work. Empowering your team fosters growth, enhances their skills, and increases their engagement and motivation.
6. **Lead by example:** Be a role model for your team. Demonstrate the behaviors and values you expect from them. Show integrity, accountability, professionalism, and a strong work ethic. Leading by example inspires and motivates your team members to perform at their best.
7. **Foster Collaboration:** Encourage collaboration and teamwork within your team. Create an environment where diverse perspectives are valued and teamwork is promoted. Facilitate effective communication, encourage

knowledge sharing, and foster a supportive and inclusive culture.
8. **Develop Coaching Skills:** Become a coach to your team members. Support their growth and development by providing guidance, mentoring, and constructive feedback. Help them identify and leverage their strengths, and provide opportunities for learning and skill enhancement.
9. **Set clear goals and expectations:** Clearly define goals and expectations for your team. Ensure that they are specific, measurable, achievable, relevant, and time-bound (SMART). Communicate these goals and expectations effectively, and provide the necessary resources and support to help your team achieve them.
10. **Practice self-reflection:** Regularly reflect on your leadership performance and actions. Assess your strengths, weaknesses, and areas for improvement. Consider the impact of your leadership style on your team and the overall organization. Adjust your approach as needed, and strive for continuous growth and improvement.

By implementing these tips and consistently investing in your leadership development, you can enhance your leadership skills and create a positive and productive work environment for your team.

If you're wondering how to improve your leadership skills, these strategies can help you get started.

1. *Assess your leadership style.*
2. *Set Clear Goals.*
3. *Grow Your Network. ...*
4. *Connect with a mentor.*
5. *Develop your emotional intelligence.*
6. *Engage in ongoing self-assessment.*
7. *Make time for self-care. ...*
8. *Identify your company's challenges.*

How do you maximize your le?

Collaborate with, and truly listen to understand, others; use a variety of influencing styles and tactics; manage conflict and resistance; and. Facilitate better conversations and become better at coaching others.

Tips to Train and Cultivate Great Leaders

1. *Start training early. Recognizing the potential in an individual early on is an*

essential component for retaining the talent that helps businesses grow.
2. *Be a mentor who leads by example.*
3. *Invest in training.*
4. *Provide autonomy.*
5. *Teach networking skills.*
6. *Promote from within.*

By implementing these tips and consistently investing in your leadership development, you can enhance your leadership skills and create a positive and productive work environment for your team.

HOW CAN YOU MASTER OR FURTHER YOUR LEADERSHIP SKILLS

MOTIVATING AND EFFECTIVE PERFORMANCE APPRAISAL

Motivating and effective performance appraisals play a crucial role in driving employee engagement, improving performance, and fostering a culture of continuous growth and development within an organization. Here's an explanation of what makes a performance appraisal motivating and effective:

1. **Clear and Specific Goals:** *Performance appraisals should be based on clear and specific goals that are aligned with the individual's role and the organization's objectives. Clearly communicate performance expectations, key result areas, and measurable targets. Well-defined goals provide employees with a sense of purpose and direction, motivating them to strive for excellence.*
2. **Regular and Timely Feedback:** *Feedback should be provided on a regular basis rather than just during the annual performance appraisal. Timely feedback allows employees to course-correct, make improvements, and build on their strengths. Provide constructive feedback that highlights both achievements and areas for improvement, focusing on specific behaviors and outcomes.*

3. **Two-Way Communication:** Effective performance appraisals involve a two-way dialogue between the employee and the manager. Encourage employees to share their perspectives, challenges, and career aspirations. Actively listen to their input, concerns, and ideas. Engaging in a meaningful conversation fosters trust, strengthens the supervisor-employee relationship, and promotes employee engagement.
4. **Recognition and Appreciation:** Recognize and appreciate employees' achievements and contributions during the performance appraisal process. Acknowledge their hard work, accomplishments, and positive impact on the organization. Genuine recognition and appreciation reinforce positive behaviors, boost morale, and motivate employees to continue performing at a high level.
5. **Development and Growth Opportunities:** Motivating performance appraisals go beyond evaluating past performance; they also focus on future growth and development. Identify areas where employees can enhance their skills, provide training opportunities, and support their professional development.

Discuss potential career paths, advancement opportunities, and ways to expand their responsibilities.
6. **Fairness and Transparency:** Ensure that the performance appraisal process is fair, transparent, and consistent across the organization. Use objective criteria and performance metrics to evaluate performance and make decisions. Employees should perceive the process as equitable and unbiased, which fosters trust and confidence in the appraisal system.
7. **Goal-Setting for the Future:** Set new goals and performance expectations for the upcoming period. Collaboratively discuss and establish goals that are challenging yet attainable. Involve employees in the goal-setting process to enhance their commitment and ownership. Clear goals provide a roadmap for employees to focus their efforts and strive for continuous improvement.
8. **Performance Improvement Plans:** If an employee's performance falls below expectations, provide support through performance improvement plans (PIPs). Clearly outline the areas that require improvement, set specific targets, and

offer guidance and resources to help the employee succeed. Regularly monitor progress and provide feedback to assist them in meeting the desired performance standards.

9. **Follow-Up and Accountability:** *Ensure that the progress made during the performance appraisal is followed up with regular check-ins and ongoing feedback. Hold employees accountable for their commitments and provide support to help them overcome challenges. Maintain an open line of communication to address any issues or concerns that may arise.*

10. **Continuous Improvement of the Process:** *Regularly evaluate and improve the performance appraisal process based on feedback from employees and managers. Seek input on the effectiveness of the process, identify areas for enhancement, and make adjustments as necessary. A continuous improvement approach ensures that the performance appraisal process remains relevant, meaningful, and motivating.*

By incorporating these elements into the performance appraisal process, organizations can create a culture of motivation, growth, and high performance, leading to improved individual and organizational outcomes.

An effective performance appraisal system provides consistent, reliable, and valid data to help managers and employees assess and improve performance.

Here are the key characteristics of an effective performance appraisal:

1. **Clear Objectives:** *The appraisal system should have clear objectives that align with the organization's goals and values. It should be designed to measure and evaluate employee performance accurately and fairly.*
2. **Defined Criteria and Standards:** *The system should establish specific criteria and performance standards against which employees' performance is evaluated. These criteria should be objective, measurable, and relevant to the job responsibilities and organizational expectations.*
3. **Regular Feedback:** *An effective performance appraisal system encourages regular feedback*

throughout the performance cycle rather than relying solely on an annual review. Managers should provide ongoing feedback to employees, highlighting strengths, identifying areas for improvement, and offering guidance and support.

4. **Two-Way Communication:** The appraisal process should facilitate open and honest communication between managers and employees. It should provide opportunities for employees to express their perspectives, concerns, and aspirations. A two-way dialogue helps build trust, enhances understanding, and promotes employee engagement.

5. **Performance Documentation:** The appraisal system should include documentation of performance-related information, such as goals, achievements, feedback, and development plans. This documentation serves as a reference for future evaluations, supports decision-making, and helps in identifying patterns and trends over time.

6. **Employee Development:** An effective appraisal system should focus not only on evaluating past performance but also

on employee development. It should provide opportunities for employees to set goals, receive training and development support, and discuss career aspirations. Development plans should be formulated to enhance employee skills and facilitate growth.
7. **Fairness and Objectivity:** The appraisal system should be fair, unbiased, and based on objective criteria. Performance evaluations should be conducted consistently across all employees, avoiding favoritism or discrimination. The process should rely on accurate and relevant data rather than personal biases.
8. **Managerial Training:** Managers involved in the performance appraisal process should receive training on how to conduct effective evaluations, provide constructive feedback, and handle challenging conversations. Training helps ensure that managers have the necessary skills and knowledge to conduct fair and meaningful appraisals.
9. **Performance Recognition and Rewards:** An effective appraisal system should recognize and reward exceptional performance. It should identify and acknowledge employees'

achievements and contributions to the organization. Recognition and rewards can include financial incentives, promotions, public acknowledgment, or opportunities for career advancement.

10. **Continuous Improvement**: An effective performance appraisal system should be regularly evaluated and improved based on feedback and organizational needs. It should adapt to changing circumstances and align with the evolving goals and strategies of the organization. Regular reviews and updates ensure that the system remains relevant, meaningful, and effective in driving performance improvement.

Overall, an effective performance appraisal system provides a structured and fair process for evaluating and developing employee performance, leading to increased motivation, productivity, and organizational success.

How do you write a motivation for a performance appraisal?

Positive phrases:

1. "You always manage your time effectively and are very well organized

in your tasks, which has shown great productivity in your work performance."
2. *"You display a strong drive to improve productivity to meet your goals. ..."*
3. *"You have a strong work ethic that speaks for itself."*

How do you motivate employees to perform?

Employees are often heavily motivated by incentives, rewards, and compensation. Offering employees incentives such as short breaks or office perks could make their lives easier and help keep them motivated. For example, a Nescafe coffee machine for the office may help them save time and money on coffee.

There are many different ways to motivate your employees to keep them engaged with your organization.

- *Keep communication lines open.*
- *Set clear goals and expectations.*
- *Create and maintain a culture of rewards and recognition.*
- *Offer mentoring opportunities.*
- *Create a positive work environment.*
- *Lead by example.*

- *Allow for autonomy.*

What is an example of motivation?

What are some examples of motivation? An example of motivation is watching an Olympic athlete and working hard in sports to become like that athlete. Other examples include working hard at achieving a degree to get a high-paying job and taking a drink of water to quench a thirst.

By incorporating these elements into the performance appraisal process, organizations can create a culture of motivation, growth, and high performance, leading to improved individual and organizational outcomes.

COMMITMENT, MOTIVATION, AND TALENT RETENTION

Commitment, motivation, and talent retention are interconnected factors that contribute to the success and sustainability of an organization. Here's an explanation of each of these elements and their relationship:

1. **Commitment**: Commitment refers to an employee's dedication and loyalty to the organization and its goals. When employees are committed, they are more likely to go above and beyond their job descriptions, invest their time and effort, and align their actions with the organization's vision and values. Commitment is built through a combination of factors, including job satisfaction, a sense of purpose, opportunities for growth, recognition, and a positive work environment.

2. **Motivation**: Motivation is the internal drive that initiates, directs, and sustains an employee's behavior towards achieving specific goals. Motivated employees are more engaged, productive, and willing to put in discretionary effort. Organizations can enhance motivation by providing meaningful work, opportunities for skill development, clear performance expectations, recognition and rewards, autonomy, and a supportive work environment.

3. ***Talent Retention**: Talent retention refers to an organization's ability to retain its top performers and high-potential employees. It involves creating an environment that attracts and keeps talented individuals within the organization, reducing turnover rates, and retaining institutional knowledge and expertise. Talent retention is crucial because losing talented employees can have significant costs, such as recruitment expenses, productivity loss, and potential negative effects on team morale.*

***Relationship**: Commitment and motivation are closely linked to talent retention. When employees feel committed and motivated, they are more likely to stay with the organization for the long term. Here's how these elements interact:*

Commitment contributes to talent retention. *When employees feel committed to the organization, they are more likely to stay and contribute their skills and expertise over time. Commitment fosters a sense of loyalty and dedication, reducing turnover rates and ensuring continuity within the organization.*

Motivation enhances talent retention. *Motivated employees are more likely to be satisfied and engaged in their work. They find fulfillment in their roles, are driven to achieve their goals, and are less likely to seek opportunities elsewhere. Motivation contributes to a positive work environment, job satisfaction, and a sense of accomplishment, all of which can lead to talent retention.*

Talent retention reinforces commitment and motivation. *When organizations actively focus on retaining their top talent, it sends a message that employees are valued and their contributions are recognized. This reinforcement of commitment and motivation creates a positive cycle, as employees feel a stronger sense of loyalty and motivation to perform well, leading to increased retention.*

To foster commitment, motivation, and talent retention within an organization, it is essential to create a supportive work culture, provide opportunities for growth and development, recognize and reward performance, and ensure open communication and transparency. By nurturing these elements, organizations can build a dedicated and motivated workforce, retain top talent, and drive long-term success.

How can organizations create a supportive work culture?

Creating a supportive work culture is crucial for fostering employee engagement, satisfaction, and productivity. Here are some key strategies organizations can implement to cultivate a supportive work culture:

1. ***Clear Communication****: Establish open and transparent communication channels throughout the organization. Encourage regular and honest communication between employees and managers, fostering an environment where ideas, concerns, and feedback are welcomed and valued. Provide opportunities for two-way communication, such as team meetings, town halls, and suggestion boxes.*
2. ***Empowerment and autonomy****: Give employees a sense of ownership and autonomy over their work. Delegate responsibility and authority, allowing employees to make decisions and contribute their unique perspectives. Empowered employees feel trusted, valued, and motivated to take initiative, leading to increased engagement and productivity.*

3. **Collaboration and Teamwork:** Encourage collaboration and teamwork among employees. Foster a culture where individuals are encouraged to share knowledge, support one another, and work together to achieve common goals. Promote cross-functional collaboration and create opportunities for employees from different departments to collaborate on projects.
4. **Recognition and Appreciation:** Recognize and appreciate employees' efforts and achievements. Implement a formal recognition program that acknowledges and rewards outstanding performance, innovation, and contributions to the organization. Encourage peer-to-peer recognition and create a culture of appreciation where employees feel valued and motivated to excel.
5. **Work-Life Balance:** Support employees in achieving a healthy work-life balance. Offer flexible work arrangements when possible, such as remote work options, flexible hours, or compressed workweeks. Promote policies that prioritize employee well-being, such as paid time off, family-friendly benefits, and wellness programs.

6. ***Professional Development**:* *Provide opportunities for continuous learning and professional development. Offer training programs, workshops, conferences, and mentorship opportunities to enhance employees' skills and knowledge. Show a commitment to employee growth by investing in their professional development and career advancement.*
7. ***Fairness and Equity**: Ensure fairness and equity in policies, procedures, and decision-making. Treat employees with respect and impartiality, regardless of their background, gender, or other characteristics. Establish clear and transparent performance evaluation processes and reward systems that are based on objective criteria.*
8. ***Managerial Support and Coaching**: Equip managers with the skills and resources to support their teams effectively. Train managers in areas such as effective communication, coaching, and conflict resolution. Encourage managers to provide regular feedback, guidance, and support to their team members, fostering a positive and supportive relationship.*

9. ***Diversity and Inclusion**: Embrace diversity and inclusion within the organization. Foster an inclusive work environment that values and respects individuals from diverse backgrounds, experiences, and perspectives. Promote diversity in recruitment, create diverse teams, and provide equal opportunities for career growth and advancement.*
10. ***Regular Feedback and Performance Management:** Implement a robust performance management system that emphasizes regular feedback and development. Provide constructive feedback to employees, highlighting their strengths and areas for improvement. Establish clear performance goals, monitor progress, and offer support and resources to help employees succeed.*

Creating a supportive work culture requires a comprehensive and sustained effort from leadership, managers, and employees at all levels. By implementing these strategies, organizations can cultivate a positive and supportive work environment that fosters employee well-being, engagement, and success.

Ways to Motivate and Retain Top Talent

1. *What motivates employees to stay?*
2. *Learning and development opportunities.*
3. *Feeling understood.*
4. *Flexible working options.*
5. *Autonomy over their work.*
6. *Perks that are actually useful.*
7. *Being kept up to date with company news.*
8. *Strong leadership.*

The Four Pillars of Employee Retention

- *Organizational Culture. Fostering a positive organizational culture is essential for employee retention. ...*
- *Employee Benefits. Offering a competitive benefits package can attract and retain top talent.*
- *Professional Development. ...*
- *Recognition and rewards.*

Here are the five main drivers of employee retention that you and your organization should focus on.

- *Factor #1: Career Development Opportunities. ...*
- *Factor #2: Work-Life Balance. ...*

- *Factor #3: Company Culture and Employee Engagement. ...*
- *Factor #4: Recognition and Appreciation. ...*
- *Factor #5: Flexibility and adaptability*

Managing resistance to change is a critical aspect of successful change management. Resistance to change is a natural human response when individuals perceive a threat or disruption to their current routines, beliefs, or work processes.

Here are some strategies to effectively manage resistance to change:

1. **Communicate Clearly**: *Provide open and transparent communication about the reasons for the change, the benefits it will bring, and the impact it will have on individuals and the organization as a whole. Address concerns and questions proactively, and ensure that communication is consistent and ongoing throughout the change process.*
2. **Involve Employees**: *Involve employees in the change process by seeking their input, feedback, and ideas. This helps them feel heard and valued, and it increases their sense of ownership and*

commitment to the change. Encourage participation in decision-making, task forces, or change implementation teams to foster a sense of empowerment.
3. **Provide Support and Resources**: Offer resources, training, and support to help employees navigate the change successfully. Provide adequate training on new processes, technologies, or skills required for the change. Offer coaching, mentoring, or additional assistance to employees who may be struggling with the transition.
4. **Address Concerns and Resistance**: Take the time to understand the concerns and fears of individuals who are resistant to change. Listen empathetically and address their concerns directly. Provide information, reassurance, and evidence to alleviate their fears and help them see the benefits of the change. Tailor your approach to each individual and address their specific needs and perspectives.
5. **Foster a Positive Change Culture**: Create a change-supportive culture by fostering open-mindedness, adaptability, and a growth mindset. Encourage learning from failures and celebrating successes during the change process. Recognize and reward

individuals and teams that embrace and contribute to the change. This helps shift the organizational mindset towards embracing change as a positive opportunity for growth.
6. **Lead by Example**: Leaders play a crucial role in managing resistance to change. Demonstrate your commitment and support for the change by modeling the desired behaviors and attitudes. Actively participate in the change process, communicate openly, and address resistance constructively. When employees see leaders embracing the change, it can help build trust and encourage others to follow suit.
7. **Break Change into Manageable Steps**: Break down the change into smaller, manageable steps or milestones. This makes the change process less overwhelming and reduces resistance. Celebrate progress at each stage to build momentum and keep employees motivated.
8. **Monitor and Adjust**: Continuously monitor the progress of the change initiative and be open to making adjustments based on feedback and lessons learned. Stay responsive to the needs and concerns of employees, and

adapt your approach as necessary to address any ongoing resistance.
9. **Celebrate Success and Recognize Efforts:** Celebrate milestones and successes achieved throughout the change process. Recognize and appreciate the efforts and contributions of individuals and teams who have embraced and supported the change. This reinforces a positive change culture and encourages others to get on board.
10. **Learn from Resistance**: View resistance as an opportunity for learning and improvement. Analyze the underlying causes of resistance and identify any gaps or areas that need further attention. Use the insights gained to refine your change management strategies and enhance future change initiatives.

By employing these strategies, organizations can effectively manage resistance to change, increase employee engagement, and facilitate successful change implementation.

GENERATIONAL CLASH: MILLENNIALS TELEWORK AND VIRTUAL TEAMS

Generational clash refers to the conflicts or differences that arise between different generations due to varying perspectives, values, and behaviors. In the context of telework and virtual teams, there can be a generational clash between millennials and other older generations.

Millennials, also known as Generation Y, generally refer to individuals born between the early 1980s and the mid-1990s and early 2000s. They have grown up in an era of rapid technological advancements and have embraced digital tools and virtual communication platforms in their personal and professional lives. As a result, many millennials are comfortable with telework and virtual teams, where employees work remotely using technology to collaborate and communicate with their colleagues.

On the other hand, older generations, such as Baby Boomers and Generation X, may have different experiences and attitudes towards telework and virtual teams. They may be more accustomed to traditional office settings and face-to-face interactions. Some of the concerns or clashes that can arise include:

1. **Communication preferences:** Millennials often prefer digital communication methods like email, instant messaging, and video conferencing. They may find it more natural to communicate through these channels, whereas older generations might prefer face-to-face or phone conversations.
2. **Work-life balance:** Millennials tend to prioritize work-life balance and flexibility. They appreciate the freedom that telework and virtual teams offer, as it allows them to have more control over their schedules. Older generations may have different expectations regarding work hours and may value a more structured work environment.
3. **Technological proficiency**: Millennials, having grown up with technology, generally have higher technological proficiency compared to older

generations. They adapt quickly to new digital tools and platforms, while older generations may require more time and training to become comfortable with these technologies.
4. **Trust and supervision:** Some older generations may have concerns about managing teleworking employees and virtual teams. They may have a preference for in-person supervision and find it challenging to trust employees who are not physically present in the office.

To overcome these generational clashes and create a harmonious work environment, it is essential to foster understanding, open communication, and flexibility. Organizations can provide training and support to help older generations adapt to telework and virtual team environments. Encouraging intergenerational collaboration and knowledge sharing can also bridge the gap and enable different generations to learn from each other's strengths and experiences.

Generational ideal work environment

Currently, only 11% of Gen Z are working remotely full-time, compared to 27% of *millennials and 42% of Gen X. Yet, despite their current work arrangements, 40% of Gen Z, 56% of millennials, and 75% of Gen X said remote work was important to them.*

The ideal work environment can vary among different generations based on their values, preferences, and experiences.

Here's a brief overview of the ideal work environment for each of the mentioned generations:

1. *Generation Z: Gen Z, born roughly between the mid-1990s and early 2010s, is the youngest generation in the workforce. They have grown up in a highly connected and digital world. For Gen Z, the ideal work environment often includes:*

Flexibility: Gen Z values flexibility in their work arrangements. They appreciate the ability to work remotely and have control over their schedules.

Technology integration: As digital natives, Gen Z expects the use of advanced technology and digital tools in the workplace to streamline processes and enhance productivity.

Collaboration: Gen Z is known for being collaborative and team-oriented. They prefer a work environment that promotes collaboration and encourages teamwork through virtual platforms and tools.

2. *Millennials:* Millennials, as mentioned earlier, were born between the early 1980s and the mid-1990s and early 2000s. Their ideal work environment typically includes the following:

Work-life balance: Millennials prioritize work-life balance and seek a flexible work environment that allows them to pursue personal interests and maintain a healthy lifestyle.

Remote work opportunities: Many millennials appreciate the option to work remotely, as it provides flexibility and eliminates commuting time and costs.

Meaningful work: Millennials often seek meaningful and purpose-driven work. They value employers who prioritize social responsibility and offer opportunities for personal and professional growth.

Collaboration and feedback: Millennials thrive in collaborative environments where they can contribute their ideas and receive regular feedback from their supervisors and colleagues.

3. *Generation X:* Gen X represents the generation born between the mid-1960s and early 1980s. Their ideal work environment typically includes the following:

Work-life balance: Similar to millennials, Gen X values work-life balance and seeks flexibility in their work arrangements to accommodate personal commitments and responsibilities.

Professional development: Gen X appreciates employers who offer opportunities for professional development and advancement. They value continuous learning and skill enhancement.

Stability and security: Having experienced economic fluctuations, Gen X often seeks job stability and benefits. They value long-term employment opportunities and job security.

Direct communication: Gen X generally prefers direct and face-to-face communication rather than relying solely on digital platforms. They appreciate open and honest communication channels.

It's important to note that these characteristics represent general trends and that individual preferences may vary within each generation. Creating an ideal work environment often involves a balance between accommodating generational preferences while considering the unique needs of employees on an individual level.

While millennials tend to value a healthy work-life balance, Gen Z tends to be more career-driven and financially motivated. So if your company's employees consist mostly of millennials and Gen Z, you would do well to focus on benefits that contribute to work-life balance and on monetary incentives.

What are generational differences?

Values and beliefs

- *Traditionalists: respect for authority, discipline, and loyalty.*
- *Baby Boomers: teamwork, stability, and commitment.*
- *Generation X: autonomy, work-life balance, and adaptability.*
- *Millennials: purposeful work, growth, and diversity.*

- *Generation Z: entrepreneurial mindset, digital fluency, and innovation.*

CONCLUSION

Theoretical and Operational Implications

The Corona-related lockdown has shifted the working world. Telework, previously seen as an exception, has become a permanent reality for many companies. Even after the health restrictions were lifted, teleworking became the new living reality. Working from home has become a routine for employees of all ages. Analyzing demographics and generational composition and tailoring a specific approach could be a key area for employers to address when shaping the future workforce. Teleworking performed right can hold myriad benefits for both employers and employees, though it is essential that employers ensure their people and culture also adapt to the new mode of working.

Companies should take inventory of their employees and try to understand the differences and similarities between generational groups. An analysis of their specific age needs and expectations toward work should be the starting point in designing a plan to optimize connectivity and productivity and, eventually, reach their full potential. We consider that an analysis of telework's impact on work-life balance, personal productivity, and health after the pandemic was relevant for shaping the future strategies of Romanian businesses.

This study's results support companies' efforts to improve the level of satisfaction among each generation of teleworkers. As a managerial tool, it may guide managers in assessing the level of employee satisfaction regarding telework. The paper acts as a support tool while trying to achieve a balance of job satisfaction while teleworking. Our study has a theoretical contribution due to its role in providing better knowledge of the effects of teleworking on Romanian employees, which *sheds light on its advantages and disadvantages, its perceived benefits, and its inconveniences.*

Based on the first objective, the hypothesis testing revealed significant differences between generational groups in terms of the scores they have reached for each of the three areas affected by telework: work-life balance, health, and productivity. The descriptive part of the quantitative research was meant to address the second objective of the study. The characteristics of teleworkers were divided into three categories (work-life balance, productivity, and health), considering the experiences of each generation with telework.

In pursuit of employees' work-life balance during telework, managers should consider flexible telework because all respondents appreciate this kind of arrangement. Baby Boomers are the ones that highly appreciate flexible telework arrangements.

This study highlights certain challenges employees faced that affected their work-life balance. All generations feel the influence of losing social and professional interaction during recent teleworking periods. Company management should take these results into account and propose team-building activities with the scope of re-establishing classic communication between employees. Alternating the work schedule from home with the one from the office can also be analyzed. These types of actions should address another struggle mentioned by the respondents, namely hard collaboration and communication with managers or teammates. Most of Generation Y indicated this. Managers should also pay attention to the technical facilities provided to telework employees. Generation Z respondents perceive relying on Wi-Fi and technology as a struggle when working remotely. Other struggles mentioned in this study are more personal ones: the increased volume of family conflicts or not being able to detach themselves from work issues outside the usual schedule. Most of Generations Y and X reported an increased volume of family conflicts. Generation X and Baby Boomers respondents indicated difficulties in detaching themselves from work issues outside the usual schedules. To respond to these impediments during telework, companies should consider offering some specialized training to prepare employees for better management of their personal lives while working from home. Some incentives should also be considered (e.g., family trips, parties with employees and their families).

If individual productivity during telework is taken into consideration, the findings of this study report that Generation Z, Y, and Baby Boomers are highly satisfied with their job during teleworking, while Generation X is just satisfied with their job. Generation Z considers the lack of commuting as the main incentive for their higher individual productivity. For Generation Y, a more personalized office environment is the main reason for being productive while teleworking. Generation X appreciates both the lack of commuting and a more personalized office environment. Baby Boomers consider that fewer interruptions from colleagues, quieter noise levels, and a more personalized office environment are the main incentives for higher individual productivity. These results can be channeled by companies to maximize individual telework employee productivity. It is desirable for companies to offer each generation of employees what they appreciate to increase their level of productivity.

Regarding health during teleworking, most of the Generation Y respondents consider having perfect health. However, the rest reported musculoskeletal problems during recent periods of teleworking. All Baby Boomers reported musculoskeletal problems, though none of them seemed affected by isolation, depression, stress, or overwork issues in contrast to the other generations. The most affected by stress and overwork issues are Generation Y respondents. Only Generation Z and Generation X appear slightly affected by metabolic, cardiovascular, gastrointestinal, or fertility disorders. Considering these results, ensuring a working environment that protects the health of employees who are involved in teleworking is very important. Of course, the employer cannot intervene in the arrangement of the workspace from home but can take care of employees' health by offering health service packages or subscriptions to various sports activities. When the employer ensures its concern about the telework employee's health, it is likely that the employee will be satisfied and become more engaged in the organization.

Limitations and Future Research Needs

One limitation of this paper is the low number of participants in the generation groups. Further research should consider a larger and more diverse number of respondents. Another limitation of the study is the fact that productivity was a self-reported measure. Future research should consider the actual productivity of telework employees.

Further research may also consider investigating more diverse organizational characteristics of telework, providing new perspectives on how it affects well-being, health, and employees' productivity. Although this paper is based on cross-cutting research, further causality conclusions could be tested using a longitudinal study project, which would allow the investigation of the long-term effects of telework.

HOW CAN YOU MASTER OR FURTHER YOUR LEADERSHIP SKILLS

It encompasses persevering through your route to achievement by using creativity, and error correction, among other skills.

A story as example

In the realm of personal growth and achievement, there exists a fundamental truth: practice makes perfect. This tale is one of perseverance, resilience, and an unwavering commitment to self-improvement. It is the story of an individual who embarked on a relentless journey of practicing and practicing until they achieved the pinnacle of success.

Our protagonist, let's call them Alex, possessed a burning desire to excel in a particular craft. It could have been playing a musical instrument, mastering a sport, or honing a skill in the realm of the arts or sciences. Whatever the pursuit, Alex understood that greatness was not an innate gift but rather an outcome of relentless practice.

The journey began with humble beginnings. Alex's initial attempts were far from remarkable. Frustration and disappointment often lingered in the air, but through sheer determination, they refused to give up. Alex realized that each attempt, no matter how imperfect, brought them one step closer to mastery.

Days turned into weeks, weeks into months, and months into years. Alex dedicated countless hours to deliberate practice. They sought guidance from mentors, devoured educational resources, and studied the techniques of accomplished practitioners. Each practice session became an opportunity for growth—an opportunity to refine their skills and push beyond their limits.

Obstacles presented themselves along the way. Moments of doubt crept into Alex's mind, questioning the feasibility of their dreams. Yet, they remained steadfast in their resolve. They embraced the setbacks as valuable lessons and turned them into fuel for their journey. With each failure, Alex discovered a new facet of their craft, inching closer to their ultimate goal.

The path was not without sacrifice. Alex made difficult choices, opting for practice over leisure and dedicating themselves to their craft while others indulged in distractions. Friends and loved ones sometimes failed to comprehend the depth of their commitment, but Alex knew that success required unwavering focus and an unyielding work ethic.

As the years passed, Alex's efforts bore fruit. Their performances became more refined, their understanding of their craft deepened, *and their skill set expanded. They began to receive recognition, applause, and accolades. The world marveled at their talent, unaware of the countless hours of practice that lay behind each exceptional display.*

Finally, the moment arrived when Alex stood on the stage of triumph. The journey of practicing upon practicing had led them to the pinnacle of success they had envisioned years ago. Their mastery had become an inspiration to others, a testament to the power of perseverance and dedication.

In retrospect, Alex realized that the journey was never solely about the destination. It was about the growth, the transformation, and the lessons learned along the way. It was about discovering the depths of their potential and pushing beyond self-imposed boundaries. The true success lay not only in the external achievements but also in the internal evolution that occurred through the relentless pursuit of excellence.

And so, the story of Alex serves as a reminder to all who dare to dream. It is a reminder that success is not an overnight phenomenon but the culmination of countless hours of practice, resilience, and an unshakable belief in one's abilities. With each deliberate step forward and each moment of practice, we inch closer to our own unique triumphs, rewriting the narrative of our lives one practice session at a time.

About The Publisher

ABOUT Frank E. Phillips OTHER BOOKS BY Frank E. Phillips MORE RESOURCES AND SOCIAL NETWORKS PROFESSIONAL SERVICES OF Frank E. Phillips

Dear reader!

"Thanks for reading! If you enjoyed this book or found it useful I'd be very grateful if you'd post a short review on Amazon. Your support really does make a difference and I read all the reviews personally so I can get your feedback and make this book even better.

Thanks again for your support!"

www.ingramcontent.com/pod-product-compliance
Lightning Source LLC
Chambersburg PA
CBHW052143220526
45471CB00004B/1504